50 Low-Fat Food Recipes for Home

By: Kelly Johnson

Table of Contents

- Grilled Chicken Breast with Herbs
- Vegetable Stir-Fry with Tofu
- Baked Salmon with Dill
- Quinoa Salad with Lemon Vinaigrette
- Turkey Chili with Beans
- Steamed Vegetables with Soy Sauce
- Greek Yogurt Parfait with Fresh Berries
- Whole Wheat Pasta Primavera
- Black Bean Soup with Cilantro
- Grilled Shrimp Skewers
- Cauliflower Rice Stir-Fry
- Oven-Baked Cod with Herbed Crust
- Lentil Salad with Balsamic Dressing
- Egg White Omelette with Spinach and Mushrooms
- Roasted Vegetable Medley
- Low-Fat Cottage Cheese with Pineapple
- Turkey Meatballs in Marinara Sauce
- Spinach and Feta Stuffed Chicken Breast
- Broccoli and Cheddar Quiche (with low-fat cheese)
- Zucchini Noodles with Marinara Sauce
- Grilled Veggie Wraps with Hummus
- Poached Halibut with Lemon-Dill Sauce
- Chickpea Salad with Cucumber and Tomato
- Baked Apples with Cinnamon
- Mushroom Barley Soup
- Turkey and Vegetable Stir-Fry
- Steamed Mussels with White Wine and Garlic
- Quinoa Stuffed Peppers
- Ratatouille
- Grilled Portobello Mushrooms with Balsamic Glaze
- Low-Fat Banana Bread
- Stuffed Bell Peppers with Lean Ground Turkey
- Baked Sweet Potato Fries
- Caprese Salad (with reduced-fat mozzarella)
- Grilled Swordfish with Mango Salsa
- Vegetable Frittata

- Whole Wheat Pita Sandwich with Turkey and Avocado
- Lemon Garlic Shrimp with Asparagus
- Spinach and Ricotta Stuffed Shells (using low-fat ricotta)
- Edamame Salad with Ginger-Sesame Dressing
- Baked Chicken Tenders
- Cucumber and Yogurt Soup
- Roasted Red Pepper Hummus
- Low-Fat Cheesecake (using Greek yogurt)
- Turkey and Bean Chili
- Grilled Eggplant with Tomato and Basil
- Baked Tilapia with Lemon-Herb Sauce
- Greek Salad (with reduced-fat feta)
- Tofu Lettuce Wraps with Peanut Sauce
- Berry Smoothie with Low-Fat Milk

Grilled Chicken Breast with Herbs

Ingredients:

- 4 boneless, skinless chicken breasts
- 2 tablespoons olive oil
- 2 cloves garlic, minced
- 1 tablespoon fresh herbs (such as rosemary, thyme, or oregano), chopped
- Salt and pepper to taste
- Lemon wedges (optional, for serving)

Instructions:

1. **Prepare the Marinade:** In a bowl, mix together olive oil, minced garlic, chopped herbs, salt, and pepper.
2. **Marinate the Chicken:** Place the chicken breasts in a shallow dish or resealable plastic bag. Pour the marinade over the chicken, making sure each breast is coated evenly. Marinate in the refrigerator for at least 30 minutes (or up to 4 hours for more flavor).
3. **Preheat the Grill:** Preheat your grill to medium-high heat.
4. **Grill the Chicken:** Remove the chicken breasts from the marinade, shaking off any excess. Discard the remaining marinade. Place the chicken on the preheated grill and cook for about 6-7 minutes per side, or until the internal temperature reaches 165°F (75°C) and the chicken is no longer pink in the center. Cooking time may vary depending on the thickness of your chicken breasts.
5. **Serve:** Once cooked through, remove the chicken from the grill and let it rest for a few minutes. Serve hot with lemon wedges on the side, if desired.
6. **Enjoy:** This grilled chicken breast with herbs pairs well with a variety of sides such as steamed vegetables, rice, or a fresh salad. It's a healthy and satisfying meal option!

Vegetable Stir-Fry with Tofu

Ingredients:

- 1 block (about 14 oz) firm tofu, drained and pressed
- 2 tablespoons soy sauce (reduced sodium if preferred)
- 1 tablespoon rice vinegar
- 1 tablespoon sesame oil (or vegetable oil)
- 2 cloves garlic, minced
- 1 tablespoon ginger, minced
- 1 onion, thinly sliced
- 1 bell pepper (any color), thinly sliced
- 1 cup broccoli florets
- 1 carrot, julienned or thinly sliced
- 1 cup snow peas, trimmed
- 1 cup mushrooms, sliced
- 2 green onions, chopped (for garnish)
- Cooked rice or noodles, for serving

Stir-Fry Sauce:

- 1/4 cup low-sodium vegetable broth or water
- 2 tablespoons soy sauce (reduced sodium if preferred)
- 1 tablespoon hoisin sauce
- 1 teaspoon cornstarch

Instructions:

1. **Prepare the Tofu:**
   - Cut the tofu into cubes or rectangles, about 1/2-inch thick.
   - In a bowl, combine 2 tablespoons of soy sauce and rice vinegar. Add tofu cubes and gently toss to coat. Let it marinate for about 15-20 minutes.
2. **Make the Stir-Fry Sauce:**
   - In a small bowl, whisk together vegetable broth or water, soy sauce, hoisin sauce, and cornstarch until smooth. Set aside.
3. **Cook the Tofu:**
   - Heat 1 tablespoon of sesame oil (or vegetable oil) in a large skillet or wok over medium-high heat. Add the marinated tofu cubes and cook for about 4-5 minutes per side, or until golden and crispy. Remove tofu from the skillet and set aside.
4. **Stir-Fry the Vegetables:**
   - In the same skillet or wok, add a bit more oil if needed. Add minced garlic and ginger, and sauté for about 30 seconds until fragrant.
   - Add sliced onion, bell pepper, broccoli florets, julienned carrot, snow peas, and mushrooms. Stir-fry for 4-5 minutes, or until vegetables are tender-crisp.
5. **Combine Tofu and Vegetables:**

- Return the cooked tofu to the skillet with the vegetables.
6. **Add the Stir-Fry Sauce:**
    - Give the prepared stir-fry sauce a quick stir, then pour it over the tofu and vegetables in the skillet.
    - Stir well to coat everything evenly. Cook for another 1-2 minutes, or until the sauce has thickened slightly and everything is heated through.
7. **Serve:**
    - Remove from heat and garnish with chopped green onions.
    - Serve immediately over cooked rice or noodles.
8. **Enjoy:**
    - This vegetable stir-fry with tofu is a delicious and nutritious dish, packed with protein and colorful vegetables. It's perfect for a quick and satisfying meal!

Baked Salmon with Dill

Ingredients:

- 4 salmon fillets, skin-on or skinless (about 6 oz each)
- Salt and pepper, to taste
- 2 tablespoons olive oil
- 2 tablespoons fresh dill, chopped (or 1 tablespoon dried dill)
- 2 cloves garlic, minced
- 1 lemon, thinly sliced
- Lemon wedges, for serving

Instructions:

1. **Preheat the Oven:** Preheat your oven to 400°F (200°C).
2. **Prepare the Salmon:**
    - Pat the salmon fillets dry with paper towels. Season both sides with salt and pepper.
    - Place the salmon fillets in a baking dish or on a baking sheet lined with parchment paper or foil.
3. **Prepare the Dill Mixture:**
    - In a small bowl, mix together the olive oil, chopped dill, and minced garlic.
4. **Coat the Salmon:**
    - Brush the dill mixture evenly over the tops of the salmon fillets.
5. **Add Lemon Slices:**
    - Place lemon slices on top of each salmon fillet. This adds flavor and keeps the salmon moist during baking.
6. **Bake the Salmon:**
    - Bake in the preheated oven for about 12-15 minutes, or until the salmon is cooked through and flakes easily with a fork. The cooking time may vary depending on the thickness of your salmon fillets.
7. **Serve:**
    - Remove from the oven and let the salmon rest for a few minutes before serving.
    - Serve hot, garnished with additional fresh dill and lemon wedges on the side.
8. **Enjoy:**
    - This baked salmon with dill is delicious served with a side of steamed vegetables, rice, or a fresh salad. It's a healthy and flavorful dish that's perfect for any occasion!

Quinoa Salad with Lemon Vinaigrette

Ingredients:

For the Salad:

- 1 cup quinoa
- 2 cups water or vegetable broth
- 1 cucumber, diced
- 1 red bell pepper, diced
- 1/2 cup cherry tomatoes, halved
- 1/4 cup red onion, finely chopped
- 1/4 cup fresh parsley, chopped
- 1/4 cup fresh mint leaves, chopped (optional)
- Salt and pepper, to taste

For the Lemon Vinaigrette:

- 1/4 cup extra virgin olive oil
- Zest and juice of 1 lemon
- 1 tablespoon honey or maple syrup (optional, for sweetness)
- 1 clove garlic, minced
- 1 teaspoon Dijon mustard
- Salt and pepper, to taste

Instructions:

1. **Cook the Quinoa:**
    - Rinse the quinoa under cold water using a fine mesh sieve.
    - In a saucepan, bring 2 cups of water or vegetable broth to a boil. Add the rinsed quinoa and reduce the heat to low. Cover and simmer for 15-20 minutes, or until the quinoa is cooked and fluffy. Remove from heat and let it cool slightly.
2. **Prepare the Vinaigrette:**
    - In a small bowl, whisk together the olive oil, lemon zest, lemon juice, honey or maple syrup (if using), minced garlic, Dijon mustard, salt, and pepper until well combined. Adjust seasoning to taste.
3. **Assemble the Salad:**
    - In a large bowl, combine the cooked quinoa, diced cucumber, diced red bell pepper, halved cherry tomatoes, finely chopped red onion, chopped parsley, and chopped mint leaves (if using).
4. **Add the Dressing:**
    - Pour the lemon vinaigrette over the quinoa salad. Toss gently to coat all the ingredients evenly with the dressing.
5. **Chill (Optional):**

- You can chill the quinoa salad in the refrigerator for at least 30 minutes to allow the flavors to meld together. This step is optional but enhances the taste.
6. **Serve:**
    - Serve the quinoa salad at room temperature or chilled. It makes a great side dish or a light and healthy main course.
7. **Enjoy:**
    - This quinoa salad with lemon vinaigrette is packed with fresh vegetables, herbs, and a tangy dressing that complements the nutty flavor of quinoa perfectly. It's delicious, nutritious, and perfect for any occasion!

Turkey Chili with Beans

Ingredients:

- 1 tablespoon olive oil
- 1 onion, diced
- 3 cloves garlic, minced
- 1 red bell pepper, diced
- 1 lb ground turkey (preferably lean)
- 1 tablespoon chili powder
- 1 teaspoon ground cumin
- 1/2 teaspoon paprika
- 1/4 teaspoon cayenne pepper (optional, for heat)
- Salt and pepper, to taste
- 1 can (15 oz) kidney beans, drained and rinsed
- 1 can (15 oz) black beans, drained and rinsed
- 1 can (14.5 oz) diced tomatoes
- 1 cup low-sodium chicken broth
- 1 tablespoon tomato paste
- Fresh cilantro, chopped (for garnish)
- Shredded cheese, sour cream, sliced jalapeños, or avocado (optional, for serving)

Instructions:

1. **Sauté the Aromatics:**
    - Heat olive oil in a large pot or Dutch oven over medium heat. Add diced onion and cook for 3-4 minutes until softened.
2. **Cook the Turkey:**
    - Add minced garlic and diced red bell pepper to the pot. Cook for another 2-3 minutes until the bell pepper begins to soften.
    - Add ground turkey to the pot. Cook, breaking it up with a spoon or spatula, until the turkey is browned and cooked through.
3. **Season the Chili:**
    - Stir in chili powder, ground cumin, paprika, cayenne pepper (if using), salt, and pepper. Cook for 1 minute until the spices are fragrant.
4. **Add Beans and Tomatoes:**
    - Add kidney beans, black beans, diced tomatoes (with their juices), chicken broth, and tomato paste to the pot. Stir well to combine.
5. **Simmer:**
    - Bring the chili to a boil, then reduce the heat to low. Cover and simmer for 20-30 minutes, stirring occasionally, to allow the flavors to meld together and the chili to thicken.
6. **Adjust Seasoning:**
    - Taste the chili and adjust seasoning as needed with salt and pepper.
7. **Serve:**

- Ladle the turkey chili into bowls. Garnish with fresh chopped cilantro and any optional toppings such as shredded cheese, sour cream, sliced jalapeños, or avocado.
8. **Enjoy:**
    - Serve hot and enjoy this comforting and nutritious turkey chili with beans!

This recipe can be easily customized by adjusting the level of spiciness or adding additional vegetables like corn or diced zucchini. It's a satisfying meal that's perfect for a cozy dinner or for meal prepping lunches for the week.

Steamed Vegetables with Soy Sauce

Ingredients:

- Assorted vegetables of your choice (e.g., broccoli, cauliflower, carrots, snow peas, bell peppers)
- 2 tablespoons soy sauce (reduced sodium if preferred)
- 1 tablespoon sesame oil (optional)
- 1 teaspoon rice vinegar (optional)
- 1 clove garlic, minced (optional)
- Sesame seeds, for garnish (optional)
- Green onions, chopped, for garnish (optional)

Instructions:

1. **Prepare the Vegetables:**
    - Wash and prepare the vegetables by cutting them into bite-sized pieces. Try to cut them evenly so they cook uniformly.
2. **Steam the Vegetables:**
    - You can steam the vegetables using a steamer basket over boiling water on the stove, or in a microwave-safe dish with a small amount of water and covered with a lid or microwave-safe plastic wrap. Steam until the vegetables are tender but still crisp, usually about 5-7 minutes, depending on the type and size of the vegetables.
3. **Make the Soy Sauce Dressing:**
    - In a small bowl, mix together the soy sauce, sesame oil (if using), rice vinegar (if using), and minced garlic (if using). Adjust the quantities to your taste preferences.
4. **Combine and Serve:**
    - Transfer the steamed vegetables to a serving dish.
    - Drizzle the soy sauce dressing over the vegetables and gently toss to coat them evenly.
5. **Garnish (Optional):**
    - Sprinkle sesame seeds and chopped green onions on top for added flavor and presentation.
6. **Serve Immediately:**
    - Serve the steamed vegetables with soy sauce as a side dish or a light meal.

This dish is quick to prepare and versatile. It's a great way to enjoy the natural sweetness and crunch of fresh vegetables with a savory soy sauce dressing. Adjust the ingredients and seasoning according to your preferences to make it your own!

Greek Yogurt Parfait with Fresh Berries

Ingredients:

- 1 cup Greek yogurt (plain or vanilla, depending on preference)
- 1 cup mixed fresh berries (such as strawberries, blueberries, raspberries, blackberries)
- 1/4 cup granola (optional, for crunch)
- 1 tablespoon honey or maple syrup (optional, for sweetness)
- Fresh mint leaves, for garnish (optional)

Instructions:

1. **Prepare the Berries:**
   - Wash the fresh berries thoroughly under cold water. If using strawberries, hull and slice them into smaller pieces if desired.
2. **Assemble the Parfait:**
   - In a glass or bowl, start layering the ingredients. Begin with a spoonful of Greek yogurt at the bottom.
3. **Add Berries:**
   - Add a layer of mixed fresh berries on top of the yogurt.
4. **Repeat Layers:**
   - Continue layering with yogurt and berries until the glass or bowl is almost full, ending with a layer of yogurt on top.
5. **Top with Granola:**
   - Sprinkle granola over the top layer of yogurt for added crunch and texture.
6. **Drizzle with Honey or Maple Syrup (Optional):**
   - If you prefer a sweeter parfait, drizzle honey or maple syrup over the top layer of yogurt and berries.
7. **Garnish (Optional):**
   - Garnish with fresh mint leaves for a burst of color and freshness.
8. **Serve:**
   - Serve immediately and enjoy this nutritious and satisfying Greek yogurt parfait with fresh berries!

This parfait is not only delicious but also packed with protein from the Greek yogurt, vitamins from the fresh berries, and fiber from the granola (if using). It's a versatile recipe that you can customize with your favorite fruits and toppings. Perfect for a quick breakfast, snack, or even a healthy dessert option!

Whole Wheat Pasta Primavera

Ingredients:

- 8 oz whole wheat pasta (such as penne or spaghetti)
- 2 tablespoons olive oil
- 2 cloves garlic, minced
- 1 small onion, thinly sliced
- 1 cup cherry tomatoes, halved
- 1 cup broccoli florets
- 1 cup bell peppers, thinly sliced (use a mix of colors)
- 1 cup zucchini, sliced
- 1 cup yellow squash, sliced
- Salt and pepper, to taste
- 1/2 teaspoon dried oregano
- 1/2 teaspoon dried basil
- Red pepper flakes (optional, for heat)
- 1/4 cup grated Parmesan cheese (optional, for garnish)
- Fresh basil leaves, chopped (optional, for garnish)

Instructions:

1. **Cook the Pasta:**
    - Cook the whole wheat pasta according to the package instructions until al dente. Drain and set aside.
2. **Prepare the Vegetables:**
    - While the pasta is cooking, heat olive oil in a large skillet over medium heat. Add minced garlic and thinly sliced onion. Sauté for 2-3 minutes until the onion is translucent.
3. **Add Vegetables:**
    - Add cherry tomatoes, broccoli florets, sliced bell peppers, sliced zucchini, and sliced yellow squash to the skillet. Season with salt, pepper, dried oregano, dried basil, and red pepper flakes (if using). Stir well to combine.
4. **Cook Vegetables:**
    - Cook the vegetables for about 5-7 minutes, stirring occasionally, until they are tender-crisp. Adjust cooking time based on your preference for softer or crisper vegetables.
5. **Combine Pasta and Vegetables:**
    - Add the cooked whole wheat pasta to the skillet with the cooked vegetables. Toss gently to combine, ensuring the pasta and vegetables are evenly mixed.
6. **Serve:**
    - Divide the whole wheat pasta primavera into serving plates or bowls.
7. **Garnish (Optional):**
    - Garnish with grated Parmesan cheese and chopped fresh basil leaves, if desired.
8. **Enjoy:**

- Serve warm and enjoy this wholesome and flavorful whole wheat pasta primavera!

This dish is versatile, allowing you to customize it with your favorite vegetables or herbs. It's a perfect option for a satisfying and nutritious meal that's packed with fiber, vitamins, and minerals.

Black Bean Soup with Cilantro

Ingredients:

- 2 cans (15 oz each) black beans, drained and rinsed
- 1 tablespoon olive oil
- 1 onion, diced
- 2 cloves garlic, minced
- 1 red bell pepper, diced
- 1 jalapeño pepper, seeded and minced (optional, for heat)
- 1 teaspoon ground cumin
- 1 teaspoon ground coriander
- 1/2 teaspoon smoked paprika
- 4 cups vegetable broth (or chicken broth)
- 1 can (14.5 oz) diced tomatoes
- Salt and pepper, to taste
- Juice of 1 lime
- Fresh cilantro, chopped, for garnish
- Sour cream or Greek yogurt, for garnish (optional)

Instructions:

1. **Sauté Aromatics:**
   - Heat olive oil in a large pot or Dutch oven over medium heat. Add diced onion and sauté for 3-4 minutes until softened.
2. **Add Garlic and Spices:**
   - Add minced garlic, diced red bell pepper, and minced jalapeño pepper (if using). Sauté for another 2 minutes until fragrant.
3. **Add Beans and Tomatoes:**
   - Add drained and rinsed black beans, ground cumin, ground coriander, smoked paprika, vegetable broth (or chicken broth), and diced tomatoes (with their juices) to the pot. Stir well to combine.
4. **Simmer:**
   - Bring the soup to a boil, then reduce the heat to low. Cover and simmer for about 20-25 minutes, stirring occasionally, to allow the flavors to meld together.
5. **Blend (Optional):**
   - For a smoother consistency, you can use an immersion blender to blend part of the soup directly in the pot. Alternatively, transfer a portion of the soup to a blender, blend until smooth, and return it to the pot.
6. **Season and Finish:**
   - Season the soup with salt, pepper, and lime juice to taste. Adjust seasoning as needed.
7. **Serve:**
   - Ladle the black bean soup into bowls. Garnish with chopped fresh cilantro and a dollop of sour cream or Greek yogurt if desired.

8. **Enjoy:**
    - Serve hot and enjoy this flavorful and nutritious black bean soup with cilantro!

This soup is rich in protein and fiber from the black beans, and the combination of spices and cilantro adds depth and freshness to the dish. It's perfect for a cozy meal at home and can be easily customized with your favorite toppings or additional vegetables.

Grilled Shrimp Skewers

Ingredients:

- 1 lb large shrimp, peeled and deveined
- 2 tablespoons olive oil
- 2 cloves garlic, minced
- 1 teaspoon paprika
- 1/2 teaspoon ground cumin
- 1/2 teaspoon dried oregano
- 1/4 teaspoon cayenne pepper (optional, for heat)
- Salt and pepper, to taste
- 1 lemon, juiced
- Wooden or metal skewers (if using wooden skewers, soak them in water for 30 minutes before grilling)

Instructions:

1. **Prepare the Shrimp:**
   - If using wooden skewers, soak them in water for 30 minutes to prevent burning while grilling.
   - In a bowl, combine olive oil, minced garlic, paprika, ground cumin, dried oregano, cayenne pepper (if using), salt, pepper, and lemon juice. Mix well.
2. **Marinate the Shrimp:**
   - Add the peeled and deveined shrimp to the marinade. Toss to coat the shrimp evenly. Marinate in the refrigerator for at least 15-20 minutes to allow the flavors to meld.
3. **Thread the Shrimp onto Skewers:**
   - Preheat your grill to medium-high heat.
   - Thread the marinated shrimp onto skewers, evenly distributing them.
4. **Grill the Shrimp:**
   - Place the shrimp skewers on the preheated grill. Grill for about 2-3 minutes per side, or until the shrimp turn pink and opaque. Be careful not to overcook the shrimp, as they can become rubbery.
5. **Serve:**
   - Remove the grilled shrimp skewers from the grill and transfer them to a serving platter.
   - Garnish with fresh chopped parsley or cilantro if desired.
6. **Enjoy:**
   - Serve the grilled shrimp skewers hot as an appetizer, main dish, or as part of a seafood platter. They pair well with a side of rice, salad, or grilled vegetables.

Grilled shrimp skewers are quick to make and packed with flavor. They're perfect for outdoor gatherings or a quick weeknight dinner. Adjust the seasoning and spice level to your preference for a dish that suits your taste buds!

Cauliflower Rice Stir-Fry

Ingredients:

- 1 head of cauliflower
- 2 tablespoons vegetable oil or olive oil
- 1 onion, finely chopped
- 2 cloves garlic, minced
- 1 bell pepper, diced (any color)
- 1 carrot, peeled and diced
- 1 cup frozen peas
- 2 eggs, beaten (optional)
- 3 tablespoons soy sauce (reduced sodium if preferred)
- 1 tablespoon oyster sauce (optional)
- 1 teaspoon sesame oil
- Salt and pepper, to taste
- Green onions, chopped, for garnish (optional)
- Sesame seeds, for garnish (optional)

Instructions:

1. **Prepare the Cauliflower Rice:**
   - Remove the leaves and core from the cauliflower. Cut the cauliflower into florets.
   - Using a food processor, pulse the cauliflower florets until they resemble rice grains. Alternatively, you can grate the cauliflower using a box grater.
2. **Stir-Fry the Vegetables:**
   - Heat 1 tablespoon of oil in a large skillet or wok over medium-high heat. Add chopped onion and minced garlic. Sauté for 2-3 minutes until softened and fragrant.
   - Add diced bell pepper and diced carrot to the skillet. Stir-fry for another 3-4 minutes until the vegetables are tender-crisp.
3. **Cook the Cauliflower Rice:**
   - Push the vegetables to one side of the skillet. Add the remaining 1 tablespoon of oil to the empty side of the skillet. Add the cauliflower rice to the skillet.
   - Stir-fry the cauliflower rice for about 5-6 minutes, stirring occasionally, until it is cooked through and slightly tender.
4. **Add Frozen Peas and Eggs (Optional):**
   - If using frozen peas, add them to the skillet and stir-fry for 1-2 minutes until heated through.
   - Push the cauliflower rice and vegetables to the sides of the skillet, creating a well in the center. Pour beaten eggs into the center of the skillet. Allow the eggs to cook for a few seconds, then scramble them until fully cooked and combine with the cauliflower rice.
5. **Season the Stir-Fry:**

- Drizzle soy sauce, oyster sauce (if using), and sesame oil over the cauliflower rice. Stir well to combine and coat all the ingredients evenly. Season with salt and pepper to taste.

6. **Garnish and Serve:**
   - Remove the cauliflower rice stir-fry from heat. Garnish with chopped green onions and sesame seeds if desired.
7. **Enjoy:**
   - Serve hot as a main dish or side dish. This cauliflower rice stir-fry is flavorful, satisfying, and packed with vegetables. It's a perfect dish for those looking to incorporate more vegetables into their meals or following a low-carb diet.

Feel free to customize this recipe by adding your favorite protein such as cooked shrimp, chicken, or tofu, or by including other vegetables like broccoli or mushrooms. Adjust the seasoning and sauces according to your taste preferences for a dish that suits you perfectly!

Oven-Baked Cod with Herbed Crust

Ingredients:

- 4 cod fillets (about 6 oz each), skinless
- 2 tablespoons olive oil
- 1/2 cup breadcrumbs (preferably panko for a crispier crust)
- 1/4 cup grated Parmesan cheese
- 2 tablespoons fresh parsley, chopped
- 1 tablespoon fresh dill, chopped
- 1 tablespoon fresh chives, chopped
- 1 lemon, zest finely grated
- Salt and pepper, to taste
- Lemon wedges, for serving

Instructions:

1. **Preheat the Oven:**
    - Preheat your oven to 400°F (200°C). Line a baking sheet with parchment paper or foil for easy cleanup.
2. **Prepare the Herbed Crust:**
    - In a bowl, combine breadcrumbs, grated Parmesan cheese, chopped fresh parsley, dill, chives, and finely grated lemon zest. Mix well to combine.
3. **Coat the Cod Fillets:**
    - Pat the cod fillets dry with paper towels. Brush each fillet with olive oil on both sides. Season lightly with salt and pepper.
4. **Apply the Herbed Crust:**
    - Press the herbed breadcrumb mixture onto the top of each cod fillet, coating evenly and pressing gently to adhere.
5. **Bake the Cod:**
    - Place the coated cod fillets on the prepared baking sheet. Bake in the preheated oven for 12-15 minutes, or until the fish is opaque and flakes easily with a fork.
6. **Serve:**
    - Remove the baked cod fillets from the oven and let them rest for a few minutes before serving.
    - Serve hot with lemon wedges on the side for squeezing over the fish.
7. **Enjoy:**
    - This oven-baked cod with herbed crust is flavorful and tender, with a crispy topping that adds texture. It pairs well with steamed vegetables, rice, or a fresh salad for a complete meal.

This recipe is simple yet elegant, making it perfect for both weeknight dinners and special occasions. The combination of herbs, Parmesan cheese, and lemon zest creates a vibrant and delicious crust that enhances the mild flavor of the cod.

Lentil Salad with Balsamic Dressing

Ingredients:

- 1 cup green lentils
- 3 cups water or vegetable broth
- 1/2 red onion, finely chopped
- 1 bell pepper (any color), diced
- 1 cucumber, diced
- 1/2 cup cherry tomatoes, halved
- 1/4 cup fresh parsley, chopped
- 1/4 cup fresh basil, chopped (optional)
- 1/4 cup crumbled feta cheese (optional)
- Salt and pepper, to taste

For the Balsamic Dressing:

- 1/4 cup extra virgin olive oil
- 2 tablespoons balsamic vinegar
- 1 tablespoon Dijon mustard
- 1 clove garlic, minced
- 1 teaspoon honey or maple syrup (optional, for sweetness)
- Salt and pepper, to taste

Instructions:

1. **Cook the Lentils:**
   - Rinse the lentils under cold water. In a medium saucepan, bring 3 cups of water or vegetable broth to a boil. Add the lentils and reduce the heat to low. Simmer for about 15-20 minutes, or until the lentils are tender but still hold their shape. Drain any excess liquid and let them cool.
2. **Prepare the Vegetables:**
   - While the lentils are cooking, prepare the vegetables. Finely chop the red onion, dice the bell pepper, cucumber, and halve the cherry tomatoes. Chop the fresh parsley and basil.
3. **Make the Balsamic Dressing:**
   - In a small bowl, whisk together the olive oil, balsamic vinegar, Dijon mustard, minced garlic, honey or maple syrup (if using), salt, and pepper until well combined.
4. **Assemble the Salad:**
   - In a large bowl, combine the cooked and cooled lentils with the chopped red onion, diced bell pepper, diced cucumber, cherry tomatoes, fresh parsley, and basil (if using). Toss gently to mix.
5. **Add the Dressing:**

- Pour the balsamic dressing over the lentil salad. Toss again to coat all the ingredients evenly with the dressing.
6. **Add Optional Ingredients (if using):**
    - If desired, sprinkle crumbled feta cheese over the salad for added flavor and creaminess.
7. **Chill (Optional):**
    - You can chill the lentil salad in the refrigerator for at least 30 minutes before serving to allow the flavors to meld together.
8. **Serve:**
    - Serve the lentil salad at room temperature or chilled. It makes a delicious and nutritious dish on its own or as a side to grilled meats or fish.

This lentil salad with balsamic dressing is packed with protein, fiber, and vitamins from the lentils and fresh vegetables. It's versatile and can be customized with your favorite herbs and additional ingredients like diced avocado or olives. Enjoy this healthy and satisfying salad!

Egg White Omelette with Spinach and Mushrooms

Ingredients:

- 4 egg whites
- 1 cup spinach leaves, chopped
- 1/2 cup mushrooms, sliced
- 1/4 cup onion, finely chopped
- 1 clove garlic, minced
- 1 tablespoon olive oil or cooking spray
- Salt and pepper, to taste
- 1/4 cup shredded cheese (optional, for topping)
- Fresh herbs (such as parsley or chives), chopped, for garnish (optional)

Instructions:

1. **Prepare the Vegetables:**
   - Heat olive oil in a non-stick skillet over medium heat. Add chopped onion and minced garlic. Sauté for 2-3 minutes until the onion becomes translucent.
2. **Cook the Mushrooms and Spinach:**
   - Add sliced mushrooms to the skillet. Cook for 3-4 minutes until the mushrooms start to soften and release their moisture.
   - Add chopped spinach to the skillet. Cook for another 1-2 minutes until the spinach wilts. Season with salt and pepper to taste. Remove the vegetables from the skillet and set aside.
3. **Prepare the Egg Whites:**
   - In a bowl, whisk the egg whites until frothy. Season with a pinch of salt and pepper.
4. **Cook the Omelette:**
   - Wipe the skillet clean or use a separate non-stick skillet. Coat the skillet with cooking spray or a little olive oil and heat over medium heat.
   - Pour the whisked egg whites into the skillet, swirling to spread them evenly. Cook for 1-2 minutes until the edges start to set.
5. **Add Vegetables and Cheese (if using):**
   - Spoon the sautéed vegetables evenly over half of the omelette. Sprinkle shredded cheese on top if desired.
6. **Fold and Serve:**
   - Using a spatula, carefully fold the other half of the omelette over the filling. Cook for another 1-2 minutes until the cheese melts (if using) and the omelette is cooked through.
7. **Garnish and Serve:**
   - Slide the egg white omelette onto a plate. Garnish with fresh chopped herbs like parsley or chives if desired.
   - Serve hot and enjoy this healthy and flavorful egg white omelette with spinach and mushrooms!

This omelette is light yet filling, making it perfect for a nutritious breakfast or brunch. You can customize it by adding other vegetables like bell peppers or tomatoes, or by using your favorite herbs and spices. It's a great way to start your day with a boost of protein and vegetables!

Roasted Vegetable Medley

Ingredients:

- 1 red bell pepper, cut into chunks
- 1 yellow bell pepper, cut into chunks
- 1 zucchini, sliced into rounds
- 1 yellow squash, sliced into rounds
- 1 red onion, cut into wedges
- 1 cup cherry tomatoes
- 2 tablespoons olive oil
- 3 cloves garlic, minced
- 1 teaspoon dried thyme (or other herbs of choice, such as rosemary or oregano)
- Salt and pepper, to taste
- Fresh herbs (such as parsley or basil), chopped, for garnish (optional)

Instructions:

1. **Preheat the Oven:**
   - Preheat your oven to 400°F (200°C).
2. **Prepare the Vegetables:**
   - Cut the red bell pepper and yellow bell pepper into chunks.
   - Slice the zucchini and yellow squash into rounds.
   - Cut the red onion into wedges.
   - Leave the cherry tomatoes whole.
3. **Toss with Olive Oil and Seasonings:**
   - In a large bowl, combine all the prepared vegetables. Drizzle with olive oil and add minced garlic, dried thyme (or other herbs), salt, and pepper. Toss well to coat the vegetables evenly with the oil and seasonings.
4. **Roast the Vegetables:**
   - Spread the vegetables in a single layer on a baking sheet lined with parchment paper or foil for easy cleanup.
   - Roast in the preheated oven for 20-25 minutes, or until the vegetables are tender and slightly caramelized, stirring halfway through cooking.
5. **Garnish and Serve:**
   - Remove the roasted vegetable medley from the oven and transfer to a serving dish.
   - Garnish with fresh chopped herbs like parsley or basil, if desired.
6. **Enjoy:**
   - Serve hot as a side dish with grilled chicken, fish, or as part of a vegetarian meal. This roasted vegetable medley is flavorful, colorful, and packed with nutrients.

You can customize this recipe by adding other vegetables such as carrots, broccoli, or mushrooms, adjusting the cooking time as needed based on the vegetables you choose. It's a simple and delicious way to enjoy a variety of vegetables in one dish!

Low-Fat Cottage Cheese with Pineapple

Ingredients:

- 1 cup low-fat cottage cheese
- 1 cup fresh pineapple chunks (or canned pineapple chunks in juice, drained)
- Honey or agave syrup (optional, for drizzling)
- Fresh mint leaves, chopped (optional, for garnish)

Instructions:

1. **Prepare the Pineapple:**
   - If using fresh pineapple, peel and core it, then cut it into bite-sized chunks. If using canned pineapple, drain the pineapple chunks well.
2. **Combine Cottage Cheese and Pineapple:**
   - In a serving bowl or individual bowls, scoop the low-fat cottage cheese.
   - Add the fresh pineapple chunks on top of the cottage cheese.
3. **Optional Drizzle:**
   - If you prefer a touch of sweetness, drizzle honey or agave syrup over the cottage cheese and pineapple.
4. **Garnish (Optional):**
   - Garnish with chopped fresh mint leaves for added freshness and flavor.
5. **Serve:**
   - Serve immediately and enjoy this light and nutritious snack or meal.

Variations:

- **Add Nuts:** Sprinkle chopped nuts (such as almonds or walnuts) over the cottage cheese and pineapple for added crunch and healthy fats.
- **Spice It Up:** Sprinkle a pinch of cinnamon or a dash of ground ginger over the pineapple for a warm, spicy flavor.
- **Make it Creamier:** Mix in a spoonful of Greek yogurt or coconut yogurt with the cottage cheese for a creamier texture.

This low-fat cottage cheese with pineapple is not only delicious but also provides a good balance of protein, fiber, and natural sweetness from the pineapple. It's perfect for a quick breakfast, snack, or even a light dessert option. Adjust the sweetness and toppings according to your taste preferences for a dish that suits you perfectly!

Turkey Meatballs in Marinara Sauce

Ingredients:

For the Turkey Meatballs:

- 1 lb ground turkey (preferably lean)
- 1/2 cup breadcrumbs (panko or regular)
- 1/4 cup grated Parmesan cheese
- 1/4 cup milk
- 1 egg
- 2 cloves garlic, minced
- 1 tablespoon fresh parsley, chopped
- 1 teaspoon dried oregano
- 1/2 teaspoon salt
- 1/4 teaspoon black pepper
- Olive oil, for cooking

For the Marinara Sauce:

- 1 tablespoon olive oil
- 1 onion, finely chopped
- 2 cloves garlic, minced
- 1 can (28 oz) crushed tomatoes
- 1 teaspoon dried basil
- 1 teaspoon dried oregano
- 1/2 teaspoon dried thyme
- 1/2 teaspoon red pepper flakes (optional, for heat)
- Salt and pepper, to taste
- Fresh basil leaves, chopped, for garnish (optional)
- Cooked spaghetti or pasta of your choice, for serving

Instructions:

1. **Make the Turkey Meatballs:**
   - In a large bowl, combine ground turkey, breadcrumbs, grated Parmesan cheese, milk, egg, minced garlic, chopped parsley, dried oregano, salt, and black pepper.
   - Mix until well combined, but avoid overmixing to keep the meatballs tender.
   - Shape the mixture into meatballs, about 1 to 1.5 inches in diameter.
2. **Cook the Meatballs:**
   - Heat a drizzle of olive oil in a large skillet over medium heat.
   - Add the meatballs in batches, making sure not to overcrowd the pan. Cook for about 5-7 minutes, turning occasionally, until browned on all sides and cooked through. Transfer the cooked meatballs to a plate and set aside.
3. **Make the Marinara Sauce:**

- In the same skillet, heat another tablespoon of olive oil over medium heat.
- Add finely chopped onion and sauté for 3-4 minutes until softened.
- Add minced garlic and sauté for another 1 minute until fragrant.
4. **Simmer the Sauce:**
    - Stir in crushed tomatoes, dried basil, dried oregano, dried thyme, and red pepper flakes (if using).
    - Season with salt and pepper to taste. Bring the sauce to a simmer.
5. **Combine Meatballs and Sauce:**
    - Return the cooked meatballs to the skillet with the marinara sauce. Gently stir to coat the meatballs with the sauce.
    - Cover the skillet and let the meatballs simmer in the sauce for 10-15 minutes, allowing the flavors to meld together.
6. **Serve:**
    - Serve the turkey meatballs in marinara sauce hot, garnished with chopped fresh basil leaves if desired, alongside cooked spaghetti or pasta of your choice.
7. **Enjoy:**
    - Enjoy these flavorful turkey meatballs in marinara sauce as a satisfying main dish. They pair well with a side salad and crusty bread for a complete meal.

This recipe is versatile—you can adjust the seasonings and spices in the meatballs and sauce according to your taste preferences. It's a healthier twist on a classic comfort food dish that everyone will enjoy!

Spinach and Feta Stuffed Chicken Breast

Ingredients:

- 4 boneless, skinless chicken breasts
- Salt and pepper, to taste
- 2 cups fresh spinach leaves, chopped
- 1/2 cup crumbled feta cheese
- 2 cloves garlic, minced
- 1 tablespoon olive oil
- 1 tablespoon Italian seasoning (or a mix of dried oregano, basil, and thyme)
- 1 tablespoon butter, melted
- Lemon wedges, for serving (optional)
- Fresh parsley, chopped, for garnish (optional)

Instructions:

1. **Prepare the Chicken Breasts:**
   - Preheat your oven to 400°F (200°C).
   - Use a sharp knife to cut a pocket into the side of each chicken breast. Be careful not to cut all the way through. Season the chicken breasts with salt and pepper, both inside and out.
2. **Make the Spinach and Feta Filling:**
   - In a skillet, heat olive oil over medium heat. Add minced garlic and sauté for 1-2 minutes until fragrant.
   - Add chopped spinach to the skillet and cook for 2-3 minutes until wilted. Remove from heat and let it cool slightly.
   - Stir in crumbled feta cheese and Italian seasoning. Mix well to combine.
3. **Stuff the Chicken Breasts:**
   - Spoon the spinach and feta mixture into the pockets of the chicken breasts, dividing evenly among them. Secure the openings with toothpicks if necessary.
4. **Cook the Stuffed Chicken:**
   - Place the stuffed chicken breasts in a baking dish. Brush the melted butter over the tops of the chicken breasts.
   - Bake in the preheated oven for 25-30 minutes, or until the chicken is cooked through and reaches an internal temperature of 165°F (75°C).
5. **Rest and Serve:**
   - Remove the stuffed chicken breasts from the oven and let them rest for a few minutes before serving.
   - Serve hot, garnished with chopped fresh parsley and lemon wedges if desired.
6. **Enjoy:**
   - Enjoy this spinach and feta stuffed chicken breast as a main dish with a side of roasted vegetables, salad, or pasta. It's flavorful, satisfying, and perfect for a special dinner.

This dish is not only delicious but also versatile. You can customize the filling by adding sun-dried tomatoes, olives, or different herbs to suit your taste. It's sure to impress your family or guests with its tasty combination of ingredients!

Broccoli and Cheddar Quiche (with low-fat cheese)

Ingredients:

- 1 store-bought or homemade pie crust (9-inch), thawed if frozen
- 1 cup broccoli florets, chopped into small pieces
- 1/2 cup shredded low-fat cheddar cheese
- 4 large eggs
- 1 cup low-fat milk (or any milk of your choice)
- 1/2 teaspoon salt
- 1/4 teaspoon black pepper
- 1/4 teaspoon garlic powder
- 1/4 teaspoon onion powder
- 1/4 teaspoon paprika (optional)
- Cooking spray or olive oil, for greasing the pie dish

Instructions:

1. **Preheat the Oven:**
    - Preheat your oven to 375°F (190°C).
2. **Prepare the Pie Crust:**
    - If using a store-bought pie crust, follow the package instructions for pre-baking or use as-is. If using homemade, roll out the dough and line a 9-inch pie dish. Crimp the edges as desired.
3. **Prepare the Broccoli:**
    - Bring a small pot of water to a boil. Add the chopped broccoli florets and blanch for 2-3 minutes until bright green and slightly tender. Drain well and set aside.
4. **Assemble the Quiche:**
    - Sprinkle the shredded low-fat cheddar cheese evenly over the bottom of the pie crust.
    - Arrange the blanched broccoli florets evenly over the cheese.
5. **Prepare the Egg Mixture:**
    - In a mixing bowl, whisk together the eggs, low-fat milk, salt, black pepper, garlic powder, onion powder, and paprika (if using) until well combined.
6. **Pour the Egg Mixture:**
    - Pour the egg mixture over the broccoli and cheese in the pie crust.
7. **Bake the Quiche:**
    - Place the quiche in the preheated oven and bake for 30-35 minutes, or until the center is set and the top is golden brown.
8. **Cool and Serve:**
    - Remove the quiche from the oven and let it cool slightly before slicing and serving.
9. **Enjoy:**
    - Serve the broccoli and cheddar quiche warm or at room temperature. It's perfect for breakfast, brunch, or even a light dinner, paired with a side salad or fresh fruit.

This broccoli and cheddar quiche with low-fat cheese is flavorful, comforting, and packed with protein and vegetables. It's a versatile dish that you can customize by adding other ingredients like diced ham, spinach, or mushrooms. Enjoy this healthier version of a classic quiche!

Zucchini Noodles with Marinara Sauce

Ingredients:

- 4 medium zucchinis
- 2 tablespoons olive oil
- 2 cloves garlic, minced
- 1 can (28 oz) crushed tomatoes
- 1 teaspoon dried oregano
- 1 teaspoon dried basil
- 1/2 teaspoon dried thyme
- 1/4 teaspoon red pepper flakes (optional, for heat)
- Salt and pepper, to taste
- Fresh basil leaves, chopped, for garnish (optional)
- Grated Parmesan cheese, for serving (optional)

Instructions:

1. **Prepare the Zucchini Noodles:**
    - Wash the zucchinis and trim off the ends. Use a spiralizer to create zucchini noodles according to the manufacturer's instructions. If you don't have a spiralizer, you can use a vegetable peeler to create long, thin strips (resembling fettuccine).
2. **Make the Marinara Sauce:**
    - In a large skillet or saucepan, heat olive oil over medium heat. Add minced garlic and sauté for about 1 minute until fragrant.
    - Pour in the crushed tomatoes and stir to combine with the garlic. Add dried oregano, dried basil, dried thyme, red pepper flakes (if using), salt, and pepper. Stir well to incorporate the spices into the sauce.
    - Bring the sauce to a simmer, then reduce the heat to low. Let it simmer gently for about 15-20 minutes, stirring occasionally, to allow the flavors to meld and the sauce to thicken slightly.
3. **Cook the Zucchini Noodles:**
    - While the marinara sauce is simmering, heat a separate large skillet over medium heat. Add a drizzle of olive oil if desired (optional).
    - Add the zucchini noodles to the skillet and sauté for 2-3 minutes, stirring occasionally, until the noodles are just tender but still crisp. Be careful not to overcook the zucchini noodles, as they can become mushy.
4. **Combine and Serve:**
    - Once the zucchini noodles are cooked to your liking, remove them from the heat.
    - Pour the marinara sauce over the zucchini noodles and toss gently to coat the noodles evenly with the sauce.
5. **Garnish and Serve:**
    - Garnish with chopped fresh basil leaves and grated Parmesan cheese, if desired.

- - Serve the zucchini noodles with marinara sauce immediately as a healthy and satisfying main dish. You can also serve it as a side dish alongside grilled chicken, fish, or tofu.

Enjoy these zucchini noodles with marinara sauce as a nutritious and flavorful alternative to traditional pasta dishes. It's a great way to incorporate more vegetables into your meals while still enjoying the delicious flavors of marinara sauce!

Grilled Veggie Wraps with Hummus

Ingredients:

- 4 whole wheat or spinach wraps (large size)
- 1 zucchini, sliced lengthwise into strips
- 1 yellow squash, sliced lengthwise into strips
- 1 red bell pepper, sliced into strips
- 1 yellow bell pepper, sliced into strips
- 1 small red onion, sliced into rounds
- 1 cup hummus (store-bought or homemade)
- 2 tablespoons olive oil
- Salt and pepper, to taste
- Fresh herbs (such as parsley or basil), chopped, for garnish (optional)

Instructions:

1. **Prepare the Vegetables:**
    - Preheat a grill pan or outdoor grill over medium-high heat.
    - Toss the zucchini, yellow squash, red bell pepper, yellow bell pepper, and red onion rounds with olive oil, salt, and pepper in a large bowl until evenly coated.
2. **Grill the Vegetables:**
    - Grill the vegetables in batches on the preheated grill until they are tender and have grill marks, about 3-4 minutes per side. Remove from the grill and set aside.
3. **Assemble the Wraps:**
    - Lay out the wraps on a clean surface.
    - Spread about 1/4 cup of hummus evenly over each wrap.
4. **Add the Grilled Vegetables:**
    - Arrange a portion of the grilled vegetables in the center of each wrap.
5. **Roll the Wraps:**
    - Fold in the sides of the wraps, then roll them up tightly starting from the bottom edge, enclosing the filling.
6. **Serve:**
    - Slice the wraps in half diagonally, if desired.
    - Garnish with chopped fresh herbs, such as parsley or basil, if using.
7. **Enjoy:**
    - Serve the grilled veggie wraps with hummus immediately, either as a whole wrap or sliced for easier handling.

These grilled veggie wraps with hummus are packed with flavor and nutrients, making them a satisfying and healthy meal option. They can be customized with your favorite vegetables or additional toppings like avocado slices or feta cheese. Enjoy this delicious and wholesome dish!

Poached Halibut with Lemon-Dill Sauce

Ingredients:

- 4 halibut fillets (about 6 oz each)
- Salt and pepper, to taste
- 2 cups fish or vegetable broth (enough to cover the fish)
- 1 lemon, thinly sliced
- Fresh dill sprigs, for garnish

For the Lemon-Dill Sauce:

- 1/2 cup plain Greek yogurt
- Zest and juice of 1 lemon
- 1 tablespoon fresh dill, chopped
- 1 clove garlic, minced
- Salt and pepper, to taste

Instructions:

1. **Prepare the Poached Halibut:**
   - Season the halibut fillets with salt and pepper on both sides.
   - In a large skillet or shallow pan, bring the fish or vegetable broth to a simmer over medium heat. Add the lemon slices.
   - Carefully place the halibut fillets into the simmering broth, ensuring they are submerged. If necessary, add more broth or water to cover the fish.
   - Poach the halibut fillets for about 8-10 minutes, or until they are opaque and flake easily with a fork. Cooking time may vary depending on the thickness of the fillets. Avoid overcooking to keep the fish tender.
2. **Make the Lemon-Dill Sauce:**
   - While the halibut is poaching, prepare the lemon-dill sauce. In a small bowl, combine the Greek yogurt, lemon zest, lemon juice, chopped fresh dill, minced garlic, salt, and pepper. Mix well until smooth and creamy.
3. **Serve:**
   - Once the halibut fillets are cooked through, carefully remove them from the poaching liquid using a slotted spoon and transfer to serving plates.
   - Spoon the lemon-dill sauce over the poached halibut fillets.
   - Garnish with additional fresh dill sprigs and lemon slices if desired.
4. **Enjoy:**
   - Serve the poached halibut with lemon-dill sauce immediately, accompanied by steamed vegetables, rice, or a fresh salad.

This poached halibut with lemon-dill sauce is light, healthy, and full of bright flavors. It's perfect for a special dinner or a light lunch. Adjust the seasoning and lemon juice according to your taste preferences for a dish that suits you perfectly!

Chickpea Salad with Cucumber and Tomato

Ingredients:

- 1 can (15 oz) chickpeas (garbanzo beans), drained and rinsed
- 1 cucumber, diced
- 1 cup cherry tomatoes, halved
- 1/4 cup red onion, finely chopped
- 1/4 cup fresh parsley, chopped
- 2 tablespoons fresh mint leaves, chopped (optional)
- Juice of 1 lemon
- 3 tablespoons olive oil
- 1 clove garlic, minced
- 1/2 teaspoon ground cumin
- Salt and pepper, to taste
- Crumbled feta cheese (optional, for garnish)

Instructions:

1. **Prepare the Chickpeas:**
    - Rinse and drain the chickpeas thoroughly. Pat them dry with a paper towel if needed.
2. **Prepare the Vegetables:**
    - Dice the cucumber into small pieces.
    - Halve the cherry tomatoes.
    - Finely chop the red onion, fresh parsley, and mint leaves (if using).
3. **Make the Dressing:**
    - In a small bowl, whisk together the lemon juice, olive oil, minced garlic, ground cumin, salt, and pepper.
4. **Assemble the Salad:**
    - In a large bowl, combine the chickpeas, diced cucumber, halved cherry tomatoes, chopped red onion, fresh parsley, and mint leaves (if using).
5. **Add the Dressing:**
    - Pour the dressing over the chickpea mixture in the bowl.
6. **Toss Gently:**
    - Gently toss all the ingredients together until everything is evenly coated with the dressing.
7. **Chill (optional):**
    - For best flavor, refrigerate the chickpea salad for at least 30 minutes before serving to allow the flavors to meld together.
8. **Serve:**
    - Serve the chickpea salad with cucumber and tomato chilled or at room temperature.
    - Optionally, garnish with crumbled feta cheese before serving.
9. **Enjoy:**

- - Enjoy this refreshing and flavorful chickpea salad as a side dish, light lunch, or a main course. It's packed with protein, fiber, and fresh vegetables, making it both satisfying and healthy.

This chickpea salad with cucumber and tomato is versatile—you can customize it by adding other vegetables like bell peppers or avocado, or by adjusting the seasoning and herbs to your taste. It's perfect for meal prep and can be enjoyed on its own or as a filling for wraps or sandwiches.

Baked Apples with Cinnamon

Ingredients:

- 4 apples (such as Granny Smith, Honeycrisp, or Gala)
- 2 tablespoons unsalted butter, melted (or substitute with coconut oil for a dairy-free option)
- 2 tablespoons brown sugar (or substitute with honey or maple syrup for a healthier option)
- 1 teaspoon ground cinnamon
- 1/4 teaspoon ground nutmeg (optional)
- 1/4 cup chopped nuts (such as walnuts or pecans) (optional)
- Vanilla ice cream or whipped cream, for serving (optional)

Instructions:

1. **Preheat the Oven:**
   - Preheat your oven to 375°F (190°C).
2. **Prepare the Apples:**
   - Wash the apples and pat them dry with a paper towel.
   - Core each apple using an apple corer or a small knife, making sure to remove the seeds and tough center.
3. **Make the Filling:**
   - In a small bowl, mix together the melted butter, brown sugar (or honey/maple syrup), ground cinnamon, and ground nutmeg (if using).
4. **Fill the Apples:**
   - Place the cored apples upright in a baking dish or a rimmed baking sheet lined with parchment paper.
   - Spoon the cinnamon mixture evenly into the center of each apple, allowing some of the mixture to drizzle over the sides.
5. **Bake the Apples:**
   - Bake the apples in the preheated oven for 25-30 minutes, or until the apples are tender and the filling is bubbling and caramelized.
6. **Optional Topping:**
   - If using chopped nuts, sprinkle them over the apples during the last 5 minutes of baking to toast them lightly.
7. **Serve:**
   - Remove the baked apples from the oven and let them cool slightly.
   - Serve warm, optionally topped with a scoop of vanilla ice cream or a dollop of whipped cream.
8. **Enjoy:**
   - Enjoy these delicious baked apples with cinnamon as a cozy dessert or a sweet treat. They are perfect for cool evenings or special occasions.

This recipe is versatile—you can adjust the sweetness by using more or less brown sugar (or honey/maple syrup) according to your preference. The warm, cinnamon-spiced aroma and tender, caramelized apples make this dessert a delightful and comforting choice for any occasion!

Mushroom Barley Soup

Ingredients:

- 1 cup pearl barley, rinsed
- 8 cups vegetable or chicken broth
- 2 tablespoons olive oil
- 1 onion, finely chopped
- 3 cloves garlic, minced
- 1 lb mushrooms (cremini or button), sliced
- 2 carrots, diced
- 2 celery stalks, diced
- 1 teaspoon dried thyme
- 1 bay leaf
- Salt and pepper, to taste
- Fresh parsley, chopped, for garnish (optional)

Instructions:

1. **Prepare the Barley:**
   - Rinse the pearl barley under cold water until the water runs clear. Drain and set aside.
2. **Saute the Vegetables:**
   - In a large pot or Dutch oven, heat olive oil over medium heat. Add chopped onion and sauté for 3-4 minutes until softened.
   - Add minced garlic and sauté for another 1 minute until fragrant.
3. **Cook the Mushrooms:**
   - Add sliced mushrooms to the pot and cook for 5-6 minutes until they release their juices and begin to brown.
4. **Add Remaining Ingredients:**
   - Stir in diced carrots and celery. Cook for another 3-4 minutes until vegetables begin to soften.
   - Add dried thyme, bay leaf, salt, and pepper. Stir well to combine.
5. **Simmer the Soup:**
   - Pour in the vegetable or chicken broth and bring the mixture to a boil.
   - Once boiling, reduce the heat to low and simmer, partially covered, for about 30 minutes or until the vegetables are tender and the barley is cooked through.
6. **Adjust Seasoning:**
   - Taste and adjust seasoning with additional salt and pepper if needed.
7. **Serve:**
   - Ladle the mushroom barley soup into bowls. Garnish with chopped fresh parsley if desired.
8. **Enjoy:**
   - Serve hot and enjoy this hearty mushroom barley soup as a satisfying and nutritious meal. It pairs well with crusty bread or a side salad.

This mushroom barley soup is rich in flavor and texture, making it a comforting choice for lunch or dinner. The combination of earthy mushrooms, hearty barley, and aromatic herbs creates a soup that's both filling and delicious. Plus, it's perfect for making ahead and reheating for quick meals throughout the week!

Turkey and Vegetable Stir-Fry

Ingredients:

- 1 lb turkey breast or turkey tenderloin, thinly sliced
- 2 tablespoons soy sauce (low-sodium preferred)
- 1 tablespoon oyster sauce
- 1 tablespoon hoisin sauce
- 1 tablespoon cornstarch
- 1 tablespoon vegetable oil
- 1 onion, sliced
- 2 bell peppers (any color), sliced
- 1 cup broccoli florets
- 1 cup snap peas, trimmed
- 2 cloves garlic, minced
- 1-inch piece ginger, minced
- Salt and pepper, to taste
- Cooked rice or noodles, for serving

Instructions:

1. **Prepare the Turkey:**
    - In a bowl, combine the sliced turkey with soy sauce, oyster sauce, hoisin sauce, and cornstarch. Mix well and let it marinate for about 15-20 minutes.
2. **Heat the Oil:**
    - Heat vegetable oil in a large skillet or wok over medium-high heat.
3. **Stir-Fry the Turkey:**
    - Add the marinated turkey slices to the hot skillet. Stir-fry for 3-4 minutes until the turkey is browned and cooked through. Remove the turkey from the skillet and set aside.
4. **Cook the Vegetables:**
    - In the same skillet, add a bit more oil if needed. Add sliced onion and stir-fry for 2-3 minutes until softened.
    - Add bell peppers, broccoli florets, and snap peas to the skillet. Stir-fry for another 3-4 minutes until the vegetables are tender-crisp.
5. **Add Garlic and Ginger:**
    - Clear a space in the center of the skillet and add minced garlic and minced ginger. Cook for 30 seconds until fragrant, then mix everything together with the vegetables.
6. **Combine Everything:**
    - Return the cooked turkey to the skillet with the vegetables. Stir everything together to combine well.
7. **Season and Serve:**
    - Season the stir-fry with salt and pepper to taste. If desired, add a splash of soy sauce or oyster sauce for extra flavor.

8. **Serve:**
    - Serve the turkey and vegetable stir-fry hot over cooked rice or noodles.
9. **Enjoy:**
    - Enjoy this delicious and nutritious turkey and vegetable stir-fry as a satisfying meal. It's packed with protein, vegetables, and Asian-inspired flavors, making it a perfect choice for a quick and healthy dinner.

Feel free to customize this stir-fry by adding other vegetables like mushrooms, snow peas, or baby corn. It's a versatile dish that's great for using up any veggies you have on hand!

Steamed Mussels with White Wine and Garlic

Ingredients:

- 2 lbs fresh mussels, cleaned and debearded
- 2 tablespoons olive oil
- 4 cloves garlic, minced
- 1 shallot, finely chopped
- 1 cup dry white wine (such as Sauvignon Blanc or Pinot Grigio)
- 1/2 cup chicken or vegetable broth
- 2 tablespoons unsalted butter
- 1/4 cup fresh parsley, chopped
- Salt and pepper, to taste
- Crushed red pepper flakes (optional, for a bit of heat)
- Crusty bread, for serving

Instructions:

1. **Prepare the Mussels:**
    - Scrub the mussels under cold water to remove any grit and pull off any beards (the hairy fibers attached to the shells). Discard any mussels that are open and do not close when tapped.
2. **Saute the Aromatics:**
    - In a large pot or Dutch oven, heat olive oil over medium heat. Add minced garlic and chopped shallot, sautéing for about 1-2 minutes until fragrant.
3. **Add Wine and Broth:**
    - Pour in the white wine and chicken or vegetable broth. Bring the liquid to a simmer.
4. **Steam the Mussels:**
    - Add the cleaned mussels to the pot. Cover with a lid and steam for about 5-7 minutes, shaking the pot occasionally, until all the mussels have opened. Discard any mussels that do not open after cooking.
5. **Finish the Dish:**
    - Remove the lid and stir in the butter until melted. This will create a rich and flavorful sauce.
    - Season with salt, pepper, and crushed red pepper flakes (if using), adjusting to taste.
6. **Garnish and Serve:**
    - Stir in chopped fresh parsley for added freshness and color.
    - Serve the steamed mussels immediately in bowls, along with crusty bread for soaking up the delicious broth.
7. **Enjoy:**
    - Enjoy these steamed mussels with white wine and garlic as a delightful appetizer or main course. The combination of flavors from the wine, garlic, and broth complements the sweetness of the mussels perfectly.

This dish is perfect for entertaining guests or for a special dinner at home. It's quick to prepare and impressive in presentation, making it a favorite among seafood lovers!

Quinoa Stuffed Peppers

Ingredients:

- 4 large bell peppers (any color), tops cut off and seeds removed
- 1 cup quinoa, rinsed
- 2 cups vegetable broth or water
- 1 tablespoon olive oil
- 1 onion, finely chopped
- 2 cloves garlic, minced
- 1 zucchini, diced
- 1 cup cherry tomatoes, halved
- 1/2 cup corn kernels (fresh, canned, or frozen)
- 1 can (15 oz) black beans, drained and rinsed
- 1 teaspoon ground cumin
- 1 teaspoon chili powder
- Salt and pepper, to taste
- 1/2 cup shredded cheese (such as cheddar or Monterey Jack), optional
- Fresh cilantro or parsley, chopped, for garnish

Instructions:

1. **Prepare the Quinoa:**
   - In a medium saucepan, bring the vegetable broth or water to a boil. Add the rinsed quinoa, reduce the heat to low, cover, and simmer for about 15 minutes or until the quinoa is cooked and the liquid is absorbed. Remove from heat and fluff with a fork.
2. **Preheat the Oven:**
   - Preheat your oven to 375°F (190°C).
3. **Prepare the Bell Peppers:**
   - Cut the tops off the bell peppers and remove the seeds and membranes. If needed, trim the bottoms slightly to help them stand upright in a baking dish.
4. **Saute the Vegetables:**
   - In a large skillet, heat olive oil over medium heat. Add chopped onion and sauté for 3-4 minutes until softened.
   - Add minced garlic and diced zucchini to the skillet. Cook for another 3-4 minutes until the zucchini starts to soften.
5. **Combine Ingredients:**
   - Stir in halved cherry tomatoes, corn kernels, and black beans. Cook for 2-3 minutes until heated through.
   - Add cooked quinoa to the skillet and mix well. Season with ground cumin, chili powder, salt, and pepper. Adjust seasoning to taste.
6. **Stuff the Peppers:**
   - Spoon the quinoa and vegetable mixture evenly into the hollowed-out bell peppers, pressing down gently to pack the filling.

7. **Bake the Stuffed Peppers:**
    - Place the stuffed peppers upright in a baking dish. If desired, sprinkle shredded cheese on top of each stuffed pepper.
    - Cover the baking dish with foil and bake in the preheated oven for 25-30 minutes, or until the peppers are tender and the filling is heated through.
8. **Garnish and Serve:**
    - Remove the foil from the baking dish. Garnish the quinoa stuffed peppers with chopped fresh cilantro or parsley.
9. **Enjoy:**
    - Serve the quinoa stuffed peppers hot as a nutritious and delicious main dish. They are packed with protein, fiber, and veggies, making them a satisfying meal option.

These quinoa stuffed peppers are versatile—you can customize the filling by adding other vegetables or spices to suit your taste. They also make great leftovers for lunch the next day!

Ratatouille

Ingredients:

- 1 large eggplant, diced
- 2 zucchinis, diced
- 1 yellow bell pepper, diced
- 1 red bell pepper, diced
- 1 onion, diced
- 3 cloves garlic, minced
- 4 tomatoes, diced (or 1 can, 14 oz, diced tomatoes)
- 2 tablespoons tomato paste
- 2 tablespoons olive oil
- 1 teaspoon dried thyme
- 1 teaspoon dried oregano
- Salt and pepper, to taste
- Fresh basil or parsley, chopped, for garnish

Instructions:

1. **Prepare the Vegetables:**
   - Heat olive oil in a large skillet or Dutch oven over medium heat. Add diced onion and sauté for 3-4 minutes until softened.
   - Add minced garlic and sauté for another 1 minute until fragrant.
2. **Cook the Eggplant:**
   - Add diced eggplant to the skillet. Cook for about 5 minutes, stirring occasionally, until the eggplant starts to soften.
3. **Add Zucchini and Bell Peppers:**
   - Add diced zucchinis, yellow bell pepper, and red bell pepper to the skillet. Cook for another 5 minutes, stirring occasionally, until all the vegetables are tender.
4. **Simmer with Tomatoes:**
   - Stir in diced tomatoes (or canned diced tomatoes with their juices) and tomato paste. Mix well to combine.
5. **Season and Simmer:**
   - Add dried thyme, dried oregano, salt, and pepper to taste. Stir to incorporate the herbs and seasoning into the mixture.
   - Reduce the heat to low, cover the skillet, and let the ratatouille simmer for about 20-25 minutes, stirring occasionally, until the flavors meld together and the vegetables are tender.
6. **Garnish and Serve:**
   - Remove from heat. Taste and adjust seasoning if needed.
   - Garnish with chopped fresh basil or parsley before serving.
7. **Enjoy:**
   - Serve ratatouille warm as a main dish, side dish, or over cooked rice, pasta, or crusty bread. It's delicious both hot and at room temperature.

Ratatouille is not only flavorful and hearty but also versatile. You can add other vegetables like mushrooms, carrots, or even potatoes if desired. It's a wonderful dish that celebrates the vibrant flavors of fresh vegetables in a comforting stew.

Grilled Portobello Mushrooms with Balsamic Glaze

Ingredients:

- 4 large portobello mushrooms
- 1/4 cup balsamic vinegar
- 2 tablespoons olive oil
- 2 cloves garlic, minced
- 1 teaspoon dried thyme (or 1 tablespoon fresh thyme leaves)
- Salt and pepper, to taste
- Fresh parsley, chopped, for garnish (optional)

Instructions:

1. **Prepare the Portobello Mushrooms:**
    - Clean the portobello mushrooms by wiping them with a damp cloth or paper towel to remove any dirt. Remove the stems if they are tough (you can save them for other recipes like stocks or soups).
2. **Marinate the Mushrooms:**
    - In a shallow dish or a large resealable bag, combine balsamic vinegar, olive oil, minced garlic, dried thyme (or fresh thyme leaves), salt, and pepper. Mix well.
    - Place the portobello mushrooms in the marinade, turning them to coat evenly. Allow them to marinate for at least 15-20 minutes at room temperature, or longer in the refrigerator if you prefer.
3. **Preheat the Grill:**
    - Preheat an outdoor grill or grill pan over medium-high heat.
4. **Grill the Portobello Mushrooms:**
    - Once the grill is hot, place the marinated portobello mushrooms on the grill, gill side down. Reserve the marinade for basting.
    - Grill the mushrooms for about 4-5 minutes on each side, or until they are tender and grill marks appear.
5. **Baste with Marinade:**
    - During grilling, baste the mushrooms with the remaining marinade to keep them moist and flavorful.
6. **Prepare the Balsamic Glaze:**
    - While the mushrooms are grilling, you can prepare a balsamic glaze. In a small saucepan, heat the remaining marinade over medium heat until it starts to bubble.
    - Reduce the heat to low and simmer for about 5-7 minutes, stirring occasionally, until the glaze thickens slightly. Remove from heat.
7. **Serve:**
    - Transfer the grilled portobello mushrooms to a serving platter. Drizzle with the prepared balsamic glaze.
    - Garnish with chopped fresh parsley, if desired.
8. **Enjoy:**

- Serve the grilled portobello mushrooms with balsamic glaze immediately while hot. They are delicious on their own or served over a bed of mixed greens, alongside grilled vegetables, or as a topping for burgers and sandwiches.

Grilled portobello mushrooms with balsamic glaze are not only flavorful but also versatile. They make a fantastic vegetarian main dish or a tasty addition to any meal. The combination of savory mushrooms and tangy-sweet balsamic glaze is sure to be a hit!

Low-Fat Banana Bread

Ingredients:

- 3 ripe bananas, mashed
- 1/2 cup unsweetened applesauce
- 1/2 cup plain Greek yogurt
- 1/2 cup honey or maple syrup (adjust to taste)
- 1 teaspoon vanilla extract
- 2 cups whole wheat flour or all-purpose flour
- 1 teaspoon baking soda
- 1/2 teaspoon baking powder
- 1/2 teaspoon salt
- 1 teaspoon ground cinnamon (optional)
- 1/2 cup chopped nuts or chocolate chips (optional)

Instructions:

1. **Preheat Oven and Prepare Pan:**
   - Preheat your oven to 350°F (175°C). Grease a 9x5-inch loaf pan or line it with parchment paper.
2. **Mix Wet Ingredients:**
   - In a large bowl, mash the ripe bananas with a fork or potato masher until smooth.
   - Add unsweetened applesauce, Greek yogurt, honey or maple syrup, and vanilla extract. Mix until well combined.
3. **Combine Dry Ingredients:**
   - In a separate bowl, whisk together the flour, baking soda, baking powder, salt, and ground cinnamon (if using).
4. **Combine Wet and Dry Ingredients:**
   - Gradually add the dry ingredients to the wet ingredients, mixing until just combined. Be careful not to overmix.
5. **Add Optional Ingredients:**
   - If using, fold in chopped nuts or chocolate chips until evenly distributed in the batter.
6. **Bake:**
   - Pour the batter into the prepared loaf pan and spread it evenly.
   - Bake in the preheated oven for 50-60 minutes, or until a toothpick inserted into the center of the loaf comes out clean.
7. **Cool and Serve:**
   - Remove the banana bread from the oven and let it cool in the pan for 10-15 minutes.
   - Transfer the bread to a wire rack to cool completely before slicing.
8. **Enjoy:**
   - Slice and enjoy your low-fat banana bread as a delicious and healthier treat for breakfast or as a snack.

This recipe uses applesauce and Greek yogurt to replace traditional fats like oil or butter, resulting in a moist and flavorful banana bread with reduced fat content. The natural sweetness of ripe bananas and honey or maple syrup adds sweetness without needing additional sugar. Feel free to customize with your favorite mix-ins like nuts, seeds, or dried fruits to suit your taste preferences!

Stuffed Bell Peppers with Lean Ground Turkey

Ingredients:

- 4 large bell peppers (any color), tops cut off and seeds removed
- 1 lb lean ground turkey
- 1 tablespoon olive oil
- 1 onion, diced
- 2 cloves garlic, minced
- 1 zucchini, diced
- 1 cup cooked quinoa or brown rice
- 1 can (15 oz) diced tomatoes, drained
- 1 teaspoon dried oregano
- 1 teaspoon dried basil
- Salt and pepper, to taste
- 1 cup shredded mozzarella or cheddar cheese (optional)
- Fresh parsley or basil, chopped, for garnish (optional)

Instructions:

1. **Preheat the Oven:**
    - Preheat your oven to 375°F (190°C).
2. **Prepare the Bell Peppers:**
    - Cut the tops off the bell peppers and remove the seeds and membranes. If needed, trim the bottoms slightly to help them stand upright in a baking dish.
3. **Prepare the Filling:**
    - In a large skillet, heat olive oil over medium heat. Add diced onion and sauté for 3-4 minutes until softened.
    - Add minced garlic and diced zucchini to the skillet. Cook for another 3-4 minutes until the zucchini starts to soften.
    - Add lean ground turkey to the skillet, breaking it apart with a spoon. Cook until the turkey is browned and cooked through.
4. **Combine Ingredients:**
    - Stir in cooked quinoa or brown rice, drained diced tomatoes, dried oregano, dried basil, salt, and pepper. Mix well to combine all ingredients evenly.
5. **Stuff the Bell Peppers:**
    - Spoon the turkey and vegetable mixture evenly into the hollowed-out bell peppers, pressing down gently to pack the filling.
6. **Optional: Add Cheese:**
    - If using cheese, sprinkle shredded mozzarella or cheddar cheese on top of each stuffed pepper.
7. **Bake:**
    - Place the stuffed peppers upright in a baking dish. Cover the dish with foil.
    - Bake in the preheated oven for 30-35 minutes. Remove the foil during the last 10 minutes of baking to allow the cheese to melt and the peppers to slightly brown.

8. **Garnish and Serve:**
    - Remove the stuffed bell peppers from the oven and let them cool slightly before serving.
    - Garnish with chopped fresh parsley or basil, if desired.
9. **Enjoy:**
    - Serve the stuffed bell peppers with lean ground turkey hot as a delicious and wholesome meal. They are packed with protein, vegetables, and grains, making them a nutritious option for lunch or dinner.

This recipe is versatile—you can customize the filling by adding other vegetables like mushrooms, spinach, or corn, or adjust the seasonings to suit your taste. These stuffed bell peppers are a great way to enjoy a balanced meal while incorporating lean ground turkey for a protein boost!

Baked Sweet Potato Fries

Ingredients:

- 2 large sweet potatoes, peeled or unpeeled (scrubbed clean), and cut into fries
- 2 tablespoons olive oil
- 1 teaspoon paprika
- 1/2 teaspoon garlic powder
- 1/2 teaspoon onion powder
- 1/2 teaspoon salt, or to taste
- 1/4 teaspoon black pepper
- Optional: 1/4 teaspoon cayenne pepper (for a spicy kick)
- Fresh parsley or cilantro, chopped, for garnish (optional)

Instructions:

1. **Preheat the Oven:**
   - Preheat your oven to 425°F (220°C). Line a baking sheet with parchment paper or aluminum foil for easy cleanup.
2. **Prepare the Sweet Potatoes:**
   - Peel (optional) and cut the sweet potatoes into even-sized fries, about 1/4 to 1/2 inch thick.
3. **Season the Fries:**
   - In a large bowl, toss the sweet potato fries with olive oil, paprika, garlic powder, onion powder, salt, black pepper, and cayenne pepper (if using). Ensure the fries are evenly coated with the seasonings.
4. **Arrange on Baking Sheet:**
   - Spread the seasoned sweet potato fries in a single layer on the prepared baking sheet, making sure they are not crowded. This helps them bake evenly and become crispy.
5. **Bake:**
   - Bake in the preheated oven for 20-25 minutes, flipping halfway through using a spatula. Bake until the fries are crispy on the outside and tender on the inside.
6. **Garnish and Serve:**
   - Remove the baked sweet potato fries from the oven and transfer them to a serving platter.
   - Garnish with chopped fresh parsley or cilantro, if desired.
7. **Enjoy:**
   - Serve the baked sweet potato fries hot as a delicious and healthier alternative to regular fries. They pair well with a dipping sauce like ketchup, garlic aioli, or sriracha mayo.

These baked sweet potato fries are crispy on the outside, tender on the inside, and packed with flavor from the spices. They are perfect as a side dish or a snack, and you can easily adjust the seasonings to suit your taste preferences. Enjoy this nutritious and tasty treat!

Caprese Salad (with reduced-fat mozzarella)

Ingredients:

- 2 large ripe tomatoes, sliced
- 8 oz reduced-fat mozzarella cheese, sliced
- Fresh basil leaves
- Extra virgin olive oil
- Balsamic glaze or balsamic vinegar (optional)
- Salt and pepper, to taste

Instructions:

1. **Slice the Tomatoes and Mozzarella:**
   - Slice the tomatoes and reduced-fat mozzarella cheese into similar-sized rounds, about 1/4 inch thick.
2. **Assemble the Salad:**
   - Arrange the tomato and mozzarella slices alternately on a serving platter or individual plates, overlapping them slightly.
   - Tuck fresh basil leaves between the tomato and mozzarella slices.
3. **Season:**
   - Drizzle extra virgin olive oil over the salad.
   - Season with salt and pepper to taste.
4. **Optional: Add Balsamic Glaze:**
   - For added flavor, drizzle balsamic glaze or balsamic vinegar over the Caprese salad. The sweetness of the balsamic complements the fresh flavors of the salad.
5. **Garnish:**
   - Garnish with additional fresh basil leaves for a vibrant presentation.
6. **Serve:**
   - Serve the Caprese salad immediately as a light and refreshing appetizer or side dish.

Caprese salad with reduced-fat mozzarella is a lighter version of the classic recipe, perfect for those looking to reduce their fat intake without sacrificing flavor. The combination of fresh tomatoes, creamy mozzarella, and aromatic basil creates a delightful harmony of flavors that is both simple and delicious. Enjoy this salad as a starter or alongside grilled meats or seafood for a complete meal.

Grilled Swordfish with Mango Salsa

Ingredients:

For the Swordfish:

- 4 swordfish steaks, about 6 oz each
- 2 tablespoons olive oil
- Salt and pepper, to taste
- 1 teaspoon paprika
- 1 teaspoon garlic powder
- 1 teaspoon dried oregano
- Lemon wedges, for serving

For the Mango Salsa:

- 2 ripe mangoes, peeled, pitted, and diced
- 1/2 red bell pepper, diced
- 1/4 cup red onion, finely chopped
- 1 jalapeño pepper, seeded and minced (optional, for heat)
- Juice of 1 lime
- 2 tablespoons fresh cilantro, chopped
- Salt and pepper, to taste

Instructions:

1. **Prepare the Swordfish:**
    - Preheat your grill to medium-high heat.
    - In a small bowl, combine olive oil, salt, pepper, paprika, garlic powder, and dried oregano.
    - Brush both sides of the swordfish steaks with the olive oil mixture.
2. **Grill the Swordfish:**
    - Place the swordfish steaks on the preheated grill. Grill for about 4-5 minutes on each side, or until the fish is cooked through and easily flakes with a fork. Cooking time may vary depending on the thickness of the steaks.
    - Remove the swordfish from the grill and let it rest for a few minutes before serving.
3. **Make the Mango Salsa:**
    - In a medium bowl, combine diced mangoes, red bell pepper, red onion, minced jalapeño (if using), lime juice, and chopped cilantro.
    - Season with salt and pepper to taste. Mix well.
4. **Serve:**
    - Serve the grilled swordfish steaks hot, topped with mango salsa.
    - Garnish with additional cilantro and serve with lemon wedges on the side.
5. **Enjoy:**

- Enjoy your grilled swordfish with mango salsa as a delicious and vibrant dish. The juicy sweetness of the mango salsa complements the grilled swordfish perfectly, creating a memorable meal.

This dish is not only delicious but also nutritious, packed with lean protein from the swordfish and vitamins from the mango salsa. It's perfect for a summer barbecue or any occasion where you want to impress with fresh and flavorful seafood!

Vegetable Frittata

Ingredients:

- 8 large eggs
- 1/4 cup milk or heavy cream
- Salt and pepper, to taste
- 1 tablespoon olive oil
- 1 small onion, diced
- 1 bell pepper (any color), diced
- 1 cup sliced mushrooms
- 1 cup baby spinach leaves
- 1/2 cup cherry tomatoes, halved
- 1/2 cup shredded cheese (such as cheddar, mozzarella, or feta)
- Fresh herbs, chopped (such as parsley, basil, or thyme), for garnish (optional)

Instructions:

1. **Preheat the Oven:**
    - Preheat your oven to 350°F (175°C).
2. **Prepare the Vegetables:**
    - In a large oven-safe skillet (preferably non-stick), heat olive oil over medium heat. Add diced onion and bell pepper. Sauté for 3-4 minutes until softened.
    - Add sliced mushrooms to the skillet. Cook for another 2-3 minutes until mushrooms start to release their moisture.
    - Add baby spinach leaves and cherry tomatoes. Cook for 1-2 minutes until spinach is wilted and tomatoes are slightly softened. Remove from heat.
3. **Prepare the Egg Mixture:**
    - In a large bowl, whisk together eggs, milk or heavy cream, salt, and pepper until well combined.
4. **Assemble and Cook the Frittata:**
    - Pour the egg mixture evenly over the sautéed vegetables in the skillet. Gently stir to distribute the vegetables throughout the eggs.
    - Sprinkle shredded cheese evenly over the top of the frittata.
5. **Bake the Frittata:**
    - Transfer the skillet to the preheated oven. Bake for 20-25 minutes, or until the frittata is set in the center and the edges are golden brown.
6. **Garnish and Serve:**
    - Remove the frittata from the oven and let it cool for a few minutes.
    - Garnish with chopped fresh herbs, if desired.
7. **Slice and Enjoy:**
    - Slice the vegetable frittata into wedges or squares. Serve warm as a main dish or slice into smaller pieces for a delightful appetizer or side dish.

This vegetable frittata is not only delicious but also nutritious, packed with protein and a variety of vegetables. Feel free to customize the recipe by adding your favorite vegetables, herbs, or cheeses. It's a perfect dish for using up leftover vegetables and creating a satisfying meal any time of day!

Whole Wheat Pita Sandwich with Turkey and Avocado

Ingredients:

- 2 whole wheat pitas, cut in half
- 8 oz sliced turkey breast (or leftover cooked turkey)
- 1 avocado, sliced
- 1/2 cup baby spinach leaves
- 1/4 cup sliced red onion
- 1/4 cup sliced cucumber
- 1/4 cup hummus (optional)
- Salt and pepper, to taste
- Fresh herbs (such as parsley or cilantro), chopped, for garnish (optional)

Instructions:

1. **Prepare the Ingredients:**
   - If using whole pitas, carefully cut them in half to create pockets.
   - Slice the avocado, red onion, and cucumber. Wash and dry the baby spinach leaves.
2. **Assemble the Pita Sandwiches:**
   - Gently open each pita pocket.
   - Spread a tablespoon of hummus (if using) inside each pita half, spreading it evenly.
   - Layer sliced turkey breast, avocado slices, baby spinach leaves, red onion slices, and cucumber slices inside each pita half.
3. **Season:**
   - Season the sandwich filling with salt and pepper to taste.
4. **Garnish and Serve:**
   - Garnish with chopped fresh herbs, if desired, for added flavor and presentation.
5. **Enjoy:**
   - Serve the whole wheat pita sandwiches with turkey and avocado immediately. They are perfect for a quick and nutritious lunch or dinner.

This sandwich is not only delicious but also packed with protein, healthy fats, and fiber. It's a balanced meal that can be easily customized with your favorite vegetables or additional toppings like tomatoes or sprouts. Enjoy this wholesome and satisfying whole wheat pita sandwich with turkey and avocado!

Lemon Garlic Shrimp with Asparagus

Ingredients:

- 1 lb large shrimp, peeled and deveined
- 1 bunch asparagus, trimmed and cut into 2-inch pieces
- 4 cloves garlic, minced
- Zest of 1 lemon
- Juice of 1 lemon
- 3 tablespoons olive oil
- Salt and pepper, to taste
- Crushed red pepper flakes (optional)
- Fresh parsley, chopped, for garnish

Instructions:

1. **Prepare the Shrimp and Asparagus:**
   - If the shrimp is frozen, thaw it by running under cold water. Pat dry with paper towels.
   - Trim the ends of the asparagus and cut into 2-inch pieces.
2. **Marinate the Shrimp:**
   - In a bowl, combine the shrimp with minced garlic, lemon zest, lemon juice, 2 tablespoons of olive oil, salt, pepper, and crushed red pepper flakes (if using). Toss well to coat the shrimp evenly. Let it marinate for 10-15 minutes.
3. **Cook the Asparagus:**
   - In a large skillet or frying pan, heat the remaining 1 tablespoon of olive oil over medium-high heat.
   - Add the asparagus pieces to the skillet. Season with salt and pepper. Cook for about 4-5 minutes, stirring occasionally, until the asparagus is tender-crisp. Remove the asparagus from the skillet and set aside.
4. **Cook the Shrimp:**
   - In the same skillet, add the marinated shrimp in a single layer. Cook for about 2-3 minutes on each side, until the shrimp turns pink and opaque. Be careful not to overcook.
5. **Combine and Serve:**
   - Add the cooked asparagus back into the skillet with the shrimp. Toss everything together gently to combine and heat through.
6. **Garnish and Serve:**
   - Remove from heat. Garnish with chopped fresh parsley and additional lemon slices, if desired.
7. **Enjoy:**
   - Serve the lemon garlic shrimp with asparagus immediately while hot. It pairs well with rice, quinoa, or crusty bread.

This lemon garlic shrimp with asparagus dish is light, flavorful, and perfect for a quick and healthy dinner. The combination of citrusy lemon, aromatic garlic, and tender shrimp with crisp asparagus makes it a delightful meal option any day of the week.

Spinach and Ricotta Stuffed Shells (using low-fat ricotta)

Ingredients:

- 1 box (12 oz) jumbo pasta shells
- 1 tablespoon olive oil
- 2 cloves garlic, minced
- 1 bag (10 oz) fresh spinach, chopped (or 1 package frozen spinach, thawed and drained)
- 2 cups low-fat ricotta cheese
- 1 cup shredded mozzarella cheese, divided
- 1/2 cup grated Parmesan cheese, divided
- 1 egg, lightly beaten
- 1 teaspoon dried oregano
- 1/2 teaspoon dried basil
- Salt and pepper, to taste
- 1 jar (24-26 oz) marinara sauce

Instructions:

1. **Cook the Pasta Shells:**
    - Cook the jumbo pasta shells according to the package instructions until al dente. Drain and set aside to cool slightly.
2. **Prepare the Spinach Mixture:**
    - In a large skillet, heat olive oil over medium heat. Add minced garlic and cook for about 1 minute until fragrant.
    - Add chopped spinach to the skillet. Cook for 2-3 minutes until wilted. If using frozen spinach, ensure it is thawed and well-drained before adding to the skillet.
3. **Make the Ricotta Filling:**
    - In a large bowl, combine low-fat ricotta cheese, 3/4 cup shredded mozzarella cheese, 1/4 cup grated Parmesan cheese, beaten egg, dried oregano, dried basil, salt, and pepper. Mix well.
    - Add the cooked spinach mixture to the ricotta mixture. Stir until everything is evenly combined.
4. **Stuff the Pasta Shells:**
    - Preheat your oven to 375°F (190°C). Grease a 9x13-inch baking dish with olive oil or non-stick spray.
    - Spoon a generous amount of the spinach and ricotta mixture into each cooked pasta shell. Arrange the stuffed shells in the prepared baking dish.
5. **Assemble and Bake:**
    - Pour the marinara sauce evenly over the stuffed shells in the baking dish.
    - Sprinkle the remaining 1/4 cup shredded mozzarella cheese and 1/4 cup grated Parmesan cheese over the top.
6. **Cover and Bake:**

- Cover the baking dish with aluminum foil and bake in the preheated oven for 25-30 minutes, or until the cheese is melted and bubbly.
7. **Serve:**
    - Remove from the oven and let it cool slightly before serving.
8. **Enjoy:**
    - Serve the spinach and ricotta stuffed shells hot, garnished with fresh basil or parsley if desired.

This dish is not only delicious and comforting but also healthier with the use of low-fat ricotta cheese. It's perfect for a family dinner or a gathering with friends, and leftovers can be easily reheated for another meal. Enjoy the creamy spinach and ricotta filling wrapped in tender pasta shells and flavorful marinara sauce!

Edamame Salad with Ginger-Sesame Dressing

Ingredients:

- 2 cups shelled edamame (cooked and cooled)
- 1 red bell pepper, thinly sliced
- 1 cup shredded carrots
- 1/2 cup thinly sliced cucumber
- 1/4 cup chopped fresh cilantro or parsley
- 2 green onions, thinly sliced
- Sesame seeds, for garnish

For the Ginger-Sesame Dressing:

- 3 tablespoons soy sauce (use low-sodium if preferred)
- 2 tablespoons rice vinegar
- 1 tablespoon sesame oil
- 1 tablespoon honey or maple syrup
- 1 tablespoon freshly grated ginger
- 1 clove garlic, minced
- 1/4 teaspoon red pepper flakes (optional, for heat)

Instructions:

1. **Prepare the Edamame:**
   - Cook the shelled edamame according to package instructions (usually boiled in salted water for 3-5 minutes). Drain and rinse with cold water to cool. Set aside.
2. **Prepare the Vegetables:**
   - In a large bowl, combine the cooked and cooled edamame, sliced red bell pepper, shredded carrots, sliced cucumber, chopped cilantro or parsley, and sliced green onions.
3. **Make the Ginger-Sesame Dressing:**
   - In a small bowl or jar, whisk together soy sauce, rice vinegar, sesame oil, honey or maple syrup, freshly grated ginger, minced garlic, and red pepper flakes (if using). Adjust seasoning to taste.
4. **Assemble the Salad:**
   - Pour the ginger-sesame dressing over the edamame and vegetable mixture. Toss gently to coat everything evenly with the dressing.
5. **Chill and Serve:**
   - Refrigerate the edamame salad for at least 30 minutes to allow the flavors to meld together.
6. **Garnish and Serve:**
   - Before serving, garnish the salad with sesame seeds for added texture and flavor.
7. **Enjoy:**

- - Serve the edamame salad with ginger-sesame dressing chilled as a refreshing and nutritious side dish or light meal.

This edamame salad with ginger-sesame dressing is packed with protein, fiber, and vitamins from the vegetables and edamame beans. The ginger-sesame dressing adds a tangy and slightly spicy kick that complements the freshness of the vegetables perfectly. It's a versatile salad that can be enjoyed on its own or paired with grilled chicken, fish, or tofu for a complete meal.

Baked Chicken Tenders

Ingredients:

- Chicken tenders (about 1 lb)
- 1 cup breadcrumbs (you can use panko breadcrumbs for extra crispiness)
- 1/2 cup grated Parmesan cheese
- 1 teaspoon garlic powder
- 1 teaspoon paprika
- 1/2 teaspoon salt
- 1/4 teaspoon black pepper
- 2 eggs
- Cooking spray or olive oil

Instructions:

1. **Preheat your oven** to 400°F (200°C). Prepare a baking sheet by lining it with parchment paper or aluminum foil, and lightly coat with cooking spray or olive oil.
2. **Prepare the coating**: In a shallow dish, combine the breadcrumbs, Parmesan cheese, garlic powder, paprika, salt, and pepper. Mix well.
3. **Beat the eggs**: In another shallow dish, beat the eggs until well combined.
4. **Coat the chicken**: Dip each chicken tender into the beaten eggs, allowing excess to drip off. Then coat the chicken in the breadcrumb mixture, pressing gently to adhere the crumbs to all sides. Place the coated chicken tender on the prepared baking sheet. Repeat with the remaining chicken tenders.
5. **Bake**: Once all chicken tenders are coated and on the baking sheet, lightly spray the tops of the tenders with cooking spray or drizzle with a bit of olive oil. This will help them crisp up in the oven.
6. **Bake in the preheated oven** for about 15-20 minutes, or until the chicken is cooked through and the coating is golden brown and crispy. The internal temperature of the chicken should reach 165°F (74°C) when measured with a meat thermometer.
7. **Serve**: Remove from the oven and let the chicken tenders rest for a few minutes before serving. They're great with your favorite dipping sauces like barbecue sauce, honey mustard, or ranch dressing.

Enjoy your homemade baked chicken tenders!

Cucumber and Yogurt Soup

Ingredients:

- 2 medium cucumbers, peeled and diced
- 2 cups plain yogurt (Greek yogurt or strained yogurt works well)
- 1-2 garlic cloves, minced
- 2 tablespoons fresh dill, chopped (you can also use mint or parsley)
- 1 tablespoon olive oil
- 1 tablespoon lemon juice (adjust to taste)
- Salt and pepper to taste
- Water or chilled broth (optional, for adjusting consistency)

Optional Garnishes:

- Extra virgin olive oil
- Fresh dill, mint, or parsley leaves
- Sliced cucumbers
- Black or green olives

Instructions:

1. **Prepare the cucumbers**: Peel the cucumbers if desired, then dice them finely. You can reserve a few slices for garnish if you like.
2. **Mix the soup base**: In a large bowl, combine the diced cucumbers, yogurt, minced garlic, chopped dill, olive oil, and lemon juice. Stir well to combine.
3. **Season**: Season the soup with salt and pepper according to your taste preferences. Remember that yogurt can reduce the saltiness, so taste and adjust accordingly.
4. **Adjust consistency (optional)**: If the soup is too thick for your liking, you can add a bit of water or chilled broth to achieve the desired consistency. Mix well.
5. **Chill**: Cover the bowl with plastic wrap or transfer the soup into a covered container, and refrigerate for at least 1 hour to allow the flavors to meld together and to chill the soup thoroughly.
6. **Serve**: Before serving, taste the soup and adjust seasoning if needed. Ladle the chilled cucumber and yogurt soup into bowls. Drizzle each serving with a little extra virgin olive oil and garnish with fresh dill, mint, or parsley leaves. You can also add a few slices of cucumber and some olives on the side for extra freshness and texture.
7. **Enjoy**: Serve cold as a refreshing appetizer or light meal, especially perfect for hot summer days.

This soup is not only delicious but also packed with nutrients from the cucumbers and yogurt, making it a healthy addition to your meal repertoire.

Roasted Red Pepper Hummus

Ingredients:

- 1 can (15 oz) chickpeas (garbanzo beans), drained and rinsed
- 1/2 cup roasted red peppers (from a jar or homemade), drained if using jarred
- 1/4 cup tahini (sesame paste)
- 2 tablespoons lemon juice (about 1 lemon)
- 1-2 garlic cloves, minced
- 1/2 teaspoon ground cumin
- 1/2 teaspoon paprika (plus more for garnish)
- 1/4 teaspoon cayenne pepper (optional, for a bit of heat)
- Salt and pepper to taste
- 2-4 tablespoons olive oil
- Water, as needed for adjusting consistency

Optional Garnishes:

- Extra olive oil
- Chopped fresh parsley or cilantro
- Toasted pine nuts or sesame seeds
- Red pepper flakes

Instructions:

1. **Prepare the chickpeas**: Drain and rinse the chickpeas thoroughly under cold water.
2. **Roast the red peppers** (if not using jarred): If you're using fresh red peppers, you can roast them over an open flame or in the oven until the skin is charred. Place them in a bowl covered with plastic wrap for 10 minutes, then peel off the skins, remove seeds, and dice.
3. **Blend ingredients**: In a food processor, combine the chickpeas, roasted red peppers, tahini, lemon juice, minced garlic, ground cumin, paprika, cayenne pepper (if using), salt, and pepper.
4. **Blend until smooth**: While the food processor is running, drizzle in 2 tablespoons of olive oil and continue to blend until the hummus is smooth and creamy. If needed, add more olive oil or a bit of water (1 tablespoon at a time) to achieve your desired consistency.
5. **Adjust seasoning**: Taste the hummus and adjust the seasoning if necessary. You can add more lemon juice, salt, or spices to suit your taste.
6. **Serve**: Transfer the roasted red pepper hummus to a serving bowl. Drizzle with a little extra olive oil and sprinkle with paprika for garnish. Optionally, garnish with chopped fresh herbs, toasted pine nuts or sesame seeds, and red pepper flakes.

7. **Enjoy**: Serve the roasted red pepper hummus with pita bread, crackers, or fresh vegetable sticks like carrots, cucumbers, or bell peppers. It's a flavorful dip perfect for parties, snacks, or as part of a Mediterranean-inspired meal.

This hummus can be stored in an airtight container in the refrigerator for up to a week. Just give it a stir before serving if any separation occurs.

Low-Fat Cheesecake (using Greek yogurt)

Ingredients:

For the Crust:

- 1 cup graham cracker crumbs (about 8-10 graham crackers)
- 2 tablespoons unsalted butter, melted
- 1 tablespoon granulated sugar (optional, adjust sweetness to taste)

For the Filling:

- 2 cups plain Greek yogurt (preferably full-fat for creaminess, but low-fat works too)
- 8 oz (1 package) reduced-fat cream cheese, softened
- 1/2 cup granulated sugar
- 2 large eggs
- 2 tablespoons all-purpose flour (optional, for texture)
- 1 teaspoon vanilla extract
- Zest of 1 lemon (optional, for extra flavor)

Instructions:

1. **Preheat your oven** to 325°F (160°C). Grease a 9-inch springform pan with cooking spray or butter.
2. **Prepare the crust**: In a medium bowl, mix together the graham cracker crumbs, melted butter, and granulated sugar (if using) until the crumbs are evenly coated. Press the mixture firmly into the bottom of the prepared springform pan. Set aside.
3. **Make the filling**: In a large mixing bowl, beat together the Greek yogurt, softened cream cheese, and granulated sugar until smooth and well combined. Add the eggs one at a time, mixing well after each addition. Stir in the flour (if using), vanilla extract, and lemon zest (if using), until everything is incorporated and the mixture is smooth.
4. **Pour and bake**: Pour the filling over the prepared crust in the springform pan. Smooth the top with a spatula.
5. **Bake in the preheated oven** for about 45-50 minutes, or until the edges are set and the center is slightly jiggly. The cheesecake should be mostly firm to the touch.
6. **Cool and chill**: Remove the cheesecake from the oven and let it cool in the pan on a wire rack for about 1 hour. Then, cover the cheesecake with plastic wrap and refrigerate for at least 4 hours or overnight to chill and set completely.
7. **Serve**: Before serving, run a knife around the edge of the pan to loosen the cheesecake. Remove the sides of the springform pan. Slice and serve the cheesecake chilled.
8. **Optional garnish**: You can garnish the cheesecake with fresh berries, a dusting of powdered sugar, or a dollop of whipped cream before serving.

Enjoy this lighter version of cheesecake that still delivers on flavor and creaminess, thanks to the Greek yogurt and reduced-fat cream cheese!

Turkey and Bean Chili

Ingredients:

- 1 tablespoon olive oil
- 1 onion, chopped
- 3 garlic cloves, minced
- 1 lb ground turkey (you can use lean or extra lean)
- 1 bell pepper, diced (any color you prefer)
- 1 can (15 oz) black beans, drained and rinsed
- 1 can (15 oz) kidney beans, drained and rinsed
- 1 can (15 oz) diced tomatoes
- 1 cup corn kernels (fresh, frozen, or canned)
- 2 tablespoons tomato paste
- 2 cups chicken broth (or vegetable broth)
- 1 tablespoon chili powder
- 1 teaspoon ground cumin
- 1 teaspoon dried oregano
- Salt and pepper, to taste
- Optional toppings: shredded cheese, sour cream, chopped cilantro, diced avocado, lime wedges

Instructions:

1. **Sauté aromatics**: Heat olive oil in a large pot or Dutch oven over medium heat. Add chopped onion and sauté for 3-4 minutes until softened. Add minced garlic and sauté for another 1 minute until fragrant.
2. **Cook ground turkey**: Add ground turkey to the pot, breaking it up with a spoon or spatula. Cook for 5-7 minutes until turkey is browned and cooked through.
3. **Add vegetables and beans**: Add diced bell pepper, drained and rinsed black beans, drained and rinsed kidney beans, corn kernels, and diced tomatoes (with their juices) to the pot. Stir well to combine.
4. **Season the chili**: Stir in tomato paste, chili powder, ground cumin, dried oregano, salt, and pepper. Mix until everything is evenly coated with the spices.
5. **Simmer**: Pour in chicken broth (or vegetable broth) and bring the mixture to a boil. Once boiling, reduce the heat to low and let the chili simmer, uncovered, for about 20-25 minutes, stirring occasionally, until it thickens to your desired consistency.
6. **Adjust seasoning**: Taste and adjust salt, pepper, and spices according to your preference. If you like a spicier chili, you can add more chili powder or a pinch of cayenne pepper.
7. **Serve**: Ladle the turkey and bean chili into bowls. Serve hot with optional toppings such as shredded cheese, sour cream, chopped cilantro, diced avocado, and lime wedges.
8. **Enjoy**: Enjoy this hearty turkey and bean chili on its own or with a side of warm cornbread for a complete meal.

This recipe is versatile, so feel free to adjust the ingredients and seasonings to suit your taste. It also freezes well, making it a great option for meal prep or leftovers.

Grilled Eggplant with Tomato and Basil

Ingredients:

- 1 large eggplant, sliced into rounds (about 1/2 inch thick)
- 2-3 tablespoons olive oil
- Salt and pepper, to taste
- 2 large tomatoes, sliced
- Fresh basil leaves
- Balsamic glaze or reduction (optional, for drizzling)
- Grated Parmesan cheese (optional, for serving)

Instructions:

1. **Preheat the grill**: Preheat your grill to medium-high heat.
2. **Prepare the eggplant**: Brush both sides of the eggplant slices with olive oil. Season with salt and pepper.
3. **Grill the eggplant**: Place the eggplant slices on the preheated grill. Grill for about 3-4 minutes per side, or until tender and grill marks appear. Cooking time may vary depending on the thickness of your eggplant slices.
4. **Assemble the dish**: On a serving platter or individual plates, arrange the grilled eggplant slices. Top each slice with a slice of tomato and a few fresh basil leaves.
5. **Drizzle and season**: Drizzle a little more olive oil over the top, and optionally, drizzle with balsamic glaze or reduction for added flavor. Season with additional salt and pepper to taste.
6. **Serve**: Optionally, sprinkle grated Parmesan cheese over the top before serving.
7. **Enjoy**: Serve the grilled eggplant with tomato and basil warm or at room temperature. It makes a wonderful appetizer, side dish, or even a light lunch when served with crusty bread.

This dish celebrates the flavors of summer with the sweetness of grilled eggplant, the freshness of tomatoes, and the aromatic basil. It's simple to prepare yet bursting with Mediterranean-inspired flavors.

Baked Tilapia with Lemon-Herb Sauce

Ingredients:

For the Tilapia:

- 4 tilapia fillets (about 6 oz each)
- Salt and pepper, to taste
- Olive oil, for drizzling

For the Lemon-Herb Sauce:

- 1/4 cup fresh lemon juice (about 2 lemons)
- Zest of 1 lemon
- 2 tablespoons unsalted butter, melted
- 2 tablespoons chopped fresh herbs (such as parsley, dill, or cilantro)
- 2 garlic cloves, minced
- Salt and pepper, to taste

Instructions:

1. **Preheat your oven** to 400°F (200°C). Lightly grease a baking dish with olive oil or non-stick cooking spray.
2. **Prepare the tilapia**: Pat dry the tilapia fillets with paper towels. Place them in the prepared baking dish. Season both sides with salt and pepper. Drizzle a little olive oil over the fillets.
3. **Bake the tilapia**: Bake in the preheated oven for 10-12 minutes, or until the fish is opaque and flakes easily with a fork.
4. **Make the lemon-herb sauce**: While the tilapia is baking, prepare the sauce. In a small bowl, whisk together the fresh lemon juice, lemon zest, melted butter, chopped fresh herbs, minced garlic, salt, and pepper.
5. **Serve**: Once the tilapia is cooked through, remove it from the oven. Spoon the lemon-herb sauce over the tilapia fillets.
6. **Garnish**: Optionally, garnish with extra chopped herbs or a lemon slice before serving.
7. **Enjoy**: Serve the baked tilapia with lemon-herb sauce immediately, accompanied by your favorite side dishes such as steamed vegetables, rice, or a salad.

This recipe is simple yet yields delicious results with the bright flavors of lemon and herbs complementing the mild tilapia. It's a great dish for a quick weeknight dinner or for entertaining guests with minimal effort.

Greek Salad (with reduced-fat feta)

Ingredients:

- 1 cucumber, seeded and chopped
- 1 red bell pepper, chopped
- 1 yellow bell pepper, chopped
- 1 pint cherry tomatoes, halved
- 1/2 red onion, thinly sliced
- 1/2 cup Kalamata olives, pitted
- 4 oz reduced-fat feta cheese, crumbled
- Fresh oregano leaves, for garnish (optional)

For the Dressing:

- 1/4 cup extra virgin olive oil
- 2 tablespoons red wine vinegar
- 1 teaspoon dried oregano
- 1 clove garlic, minced
- Salt and pepper, to taste

Instructions:

1. **Prepare the vegetables**: In a large salad bowl, combine the chopped cucumber, red bell pepper, yellow bell pepper, cherry tomatoes, red onion, and Kalamata olives.
2. **Make the dressing**: In a small bowl, whisk together the extra virgin olive oil, red wine vinegar, dried oregano, minced garlic, salt, and pepper.
3. **Assemble the salad**: Pour the dressing over the salad ingredients in the bowl. Toss gently to combine and coat everything evenly with the dressing.
4. **Add the feta cheese**: Sprinkle the crumbled reduced-fat feta cheese over the salad.
5. **Garnish and serve**: Optionally, garnish the Greek salad with fresh oregano leaves for extra flavor and presentation.
6. **Serve**: Serve the Greek salad immediately as a side dish or as a light main course. It pairs wonderfully with grilled meats, fish, or as part of a Mediterranean-inspired meal.

This Greek salad is colorful, crunchy, and bursting with flavors from the fresh vegetables, salty olives, and tangy reduced-fat feta cheese. It's perfect for summer gatherings, picnics, or as a healthy lunch option. Enjoy!

Tofu Lettuce Wraps with Peanut Sauce

Ingredients:

For the Tofu Lettuce Wraps:

- 1 block (14-16 oz) firm tofu
- 1 tablespoon soy sauce or tamari
- 1 tablespoon hoisin sauce
- 1 tablespoon rice vinegar
- 1 teaspoon sesame oil
- 1 tablespoon vegetable oil
- 2 cloves garlic, minced
- 1 teaspoon grated ginger
- 1/2 cup shredded carrots
- 1/2 cup chopped bell peppers (any color)
- 1/4 cup chopped green onions
- Fresh lettuce leaves (such as butter lettuce or iceberg lettuce), washed and dried

For the Peanut Sauce:

- 1/4 cup creamy peanut butter
- 2 tablespoons soy sauce or tamari
- 1 tablespoon rice vinegar
- 1 tablespoon honey or maple syrup
- 1 clove garlic, minced
- 1 teaspoon grated ginger
- 1-2 tablespoons water (to thin the sauce, if needed)

Optional Garnishes:

- Chopped peanuts
- Fresh cilantro or Thai basil leaves
- Lime wedges

Instructions:

1. **Prepare the tofu**: Press the tofu to remove excess moisture. You can do this by wrapping the tofu block in paper towels or a clean kitchen towel, placing it on a plate, and placing a heavy object (like a cast iron skillet or books) on top for about 15-20 minutes. Then, dice the tofu into small cubes.
2. **Make the marinade**: In a small bowl, mix together soy sauce (or tamari), hoisin sauce, rice vinegar, and sesame oil. Add the diced tofu to the bowl and gently toss to coat. Let it marinate for at least 10-15 minutes.

3. **Prepare the peanut sauce**: In another bowl, whisk together peanut butter, soy sauce (or tamari), rice vinegar, honey (or maple syrup), minced garlic, and grated ginger. If the sauce is too thick, thin it out with 1-2 tablespoons of water until desired consistency is reached. Set aside.
4. **Cook the tofu**: Heat vegetable oil in a large skillet or wok over medium-high heat. Add minced garlic and grated ginger, and sauté for about 1 minute until fragrant. Add the marinated tofu cubes and cook for 5-7 minutes, stirring occasionally, until tofu is golden and slightly crispy on the edges.
5. **Add vegetables**: Add shredded carrots, chopped bell peppers, and chopped green onions to the skillet with the tofu. Cook for another 2-3 minutes until vegetables are tender-crisp.
6. **Assemble the wraps**: Spoon the tofu and vegetable mixture into lettuce leaves, creating wraps. Drizzle each wrap with peanut sauce.
7. **Garnish and serve**: Optionally, garnish with chopped peanuts, fresh cilantro or Thai basil leaves, and serve with lime wedges on the side.
8. **Enjoy**: Serve immediately and enjoy these flavorful tofu lettuce wraps with peanut sauce as a light and satisfying meal!

These tofu lettuce wraps are packed with protein and fiber, and the peanut sauce adds a creamy and savory touch. They are also customizable, so feel free to adjust the vegetables or add extra toppings according to your taste.

Berry Smoothie with Low-Fat Milk

Ingredients:

- 1 cup mixed berries (such as strawberries, blueberries, raspberries)
- 1 banana, fresh or frozen (for creaminess)
- 1 cup low-fat milk (or any milk of your choice, such as almond milk or soy milk)
- 1-2 tablespoons honey or maple syrup (optional, for sweetness)
- 1/2 cup plain low-fat yogurt (optional, for extra creaminess)
- Ice cubes (optional, if using fresh berries)

Instructions:

1. **Prepare the berries**: If using fresh berries, wash them thoroughly. If using frozen berries, you can use them directly from the freezer.
2. **Blend the ingredients**: In a blender, combine the mixed berries, banana, low-fat milk, honey or maple syrup (if using), and plain low-fat yogurt (if using). If you prefer a thicker smoothie, you can add some ice cubes as well.
3. **Blend until smooth**: Blend on high speed until all the ingredients are well combined and the smoothie reaches your desired consistency. If the smoothie is too thick, you can add a little more milk or water to thin it out.
4. **Taste and adjust**: Taste the smoothie and adjust sweetness if needed by adding more honey or maple syrup.
5. **Serve**: Pour the berry smoothie into glasses and serve immediately. Optionally, you can garnish with fresh berries or a sprig of mint.
6. **Enjoy**: Enjoy your delicious and nutritious berry smoothie with low-fat milk!

This smoothie is packed with antioxidants from the berries, potassium and fiber from the banana, and calcium from the low-fat milk, making it a healthy choice for breakfast or a snack. It's also versatile, so feel free to customize by adding protein powder, chia seeds, or other fruits according to your preferences.

www.ingramcontent.com/pod-product-compliance
Lightning Source LLC
LaVergne TN
LVHW081613060526
838201LV00054B/2231